The Real Estate Market in Ghana

I0888269

This book seeks to fill the information gap on a key emerging real estate market and demystify the perception that the market in Ghana and indeed, across sub-Saharan Africa is opaque. Drawing on decades of experience from within the market, the author presents a detailed examination of the real estate market in Ghana and its existing regulatory framework. In doing so, he provides a justification for its relevance in the subregion. It focuses on seven thematic areas – land administration, legal perspectives, market dynamics, investment potentials, market competitiveness, valuation and compensation.

This book will be a useful resource for students, academia, practitioners, real estate developers, investors and professional advisors such as valuers, surveyors, lawyers, accountants, bankers, architects, planners and engineers.

An important feature of this book is the way in which chapters are self-contained, and yet follow logically one from another. With this approach, readers can choose a reading path appropriate to their own specific needs without a loss of continuity.

Dr. Wilfred K. Anim-Odame has over 30 years of experience in the real estate industry. He is a Senior Technical Advisor at the National Development Planning Commission in Ghana. He served as the Director of the Land Valuation Division, an analogous role of the Valuer-General of the Republic of Ghana, from September 2010 to May 2012, and later as the Executive Secretary (Chief Executive Officer) of the Ghana Lands Commission between 2012 and 2018. He strategically transformed the Land Valuation Division and Lands Commission, and also championed the automation of land services delivery. He has been an external examiner for undergraduate and graduate studies as well as PhD research at the Department of Land Economy, Kwame Nkrumah University of Science and Technology (KNUST), Kumasi, Ghana, since 2011. He is a Chartered Valuer with a diverse background in land economy, property investment and finance. He is also a Member of the Royal Institution of Chartered Surveyors (MRICS) and Fellow of the Ghana Institution of Surveyors (FGhIS). He has published extensively in peer-reviewed journals, and delivered presentations at many international platforms, including the American Real Estate Society; World Bank/IMF/LSE/GWU policy workshop; International Growth Centre at the London School of Economics and Political Science; European Real Estate Society; African Real Estate Society; and International Federation of Surveyors (FIG). Dr. Anim-Odame serves as a member of the Advisory Board of the Banking, Risk and Intermediation (BRI) Research Group of Durham University Business School, United Kingdom, and is a Commonwealth Secretariat scholar.

International Real Estate Markets

The Chinese Real Estate Market
Development, Regulation and Investment
Junjian Cao

Real Estate in Italy
Markets, Investment Vehicles and Performance
Guido Abate and Guiditta Losa

Real Estate Markets and Development in South America
Understanding Local Regulations and Investment Methods in a Highly Urbanised Continent
Claudia Murray, Eliane Monetti and Camilla Ween

Real Estate in South Asia
Edited by Prashant Das, Ramya Aroul and Julia Freybote

Real Estate in Central America, Mexico and the Caribbean
Claudia Murray, Camilla Ween, Yadira Torres and Yazmin Ramirez

The Real Estate Market in Ghana
An Emerging Market in Sub-Saharan Africa
Wilfred K. Anim-Odame

For more information about this series, please visit: www.routledge.com

The Real Estate Market in Ghana

An Emerging Market in Sub-Saharan Africa

Wilfred K. Anim-Odame

Routledge
Taylor & Francis Group
LONDON AND NEW YORK

First published 2021
by Routledge
2 Park Square, Milton Park, Abingdon, Oxon OX14 4RN

and by Routledge
52 Vanderbilt Avenue, New York, NY 10017

Routledge is an imprint of the Taylor & Francis Group, an informa business

British Library Cataloguing-in-Publication Data
A catalogue record for this book is available from the British Library

Library of Congress Cataloging-in-Publication Data
Names: Anim-Odame, Wilfred K., author.
Title: The real estate market in Ghana : an emerging market in Sub-Saharan Africa / Wilfred K. Anim-Odame.
Other titles: International real estate markets (London, England)
Description: Abingdon, Oxon ; New York, NY : Routledge, 2021. | Series: International real estate markets | Includes bibliographical references and index.
Subjects: LCSH: Real estate business—Ghana. | Real property—Purchasing—Ghana. | Real property—Ghana—Finance.
Classification: LCC HD1022 .A77 2021 (print) | LCC HD1022 (ebook) | DDC 333.3309667—dc23
LC record available at https://lccn.loc.gov/2020044671
LC ebook record available at https://lccn.loc.gov/2020044672

ISBN: 978-0-367-64692-9 (hbk)
ISBN: 978-0-367-67252-2 (pbk)
ISBN: 978-1-003-13047-5 (ebk)

To the celebration of Madam Monica Abena Donkor, my loving mother, to whom I owed a debt I could never repay.

Contents

Tables

Figures

Acknowledgements

I want to first thank Evelyn, my wife, and Genevieve, Michelle and Wilfred (Jr.), my children, for their love and great support. Over the years, some other people have played priceless roles in my life as mentors, counsellors and friends to whom I owe so much gratitude. For many of these people, it has been a long-standing relationship.

I sincerely express my deep appreciation to Professor Tony Key of Cass Business School, City University of London, UK, who supervised my PhD research and laid the foundation for this book. My sincere thank you to Professor Simon Stevenson, currently with the University of Washington, Seattle, USA, who was the second supervisor of my PhD research. I also wish to gratefully acknowledge Professor Dennis Philip of Durham University, UK, for providing the Foreword. Indeed, I cannot better express my deep appreciation to him.

I am sincerely indebted to Professor G. K. A. Ofosu-Amaah, former Dean, Faculty of Law, University of Ghana, Accra, Ghana, for being a strong pillar in my life and of great support in my career development and scholarly pursuits. At the end of my tenure as the Executive Secretary of the Ghana Lands Commission in June 2018, he requested for a codified and bound copy of my research works. On the day of presentation, a week after, he asked for an autograph and quizzed me when the main book was going to be ready. That was, indeed, a wake-up call. I am also thankful to Edward Cofie, Senior Trust Administrator at BNY Mellon, New York, USA, and formerly of the Ghana Commercial Bank and Land Valuation Board, Accra, Ghana. As a mentor and a friend, he did not only see the potential in me as far back in 1988 at the then University of Science and Technology, Kumasi, Ghana, but also supervised my work at the Land Valuation Board in Accra, which culminated in my professional competence qualification as a Valuer in 1992. In April 2019, he further corroborated the belief of Professor Ofosu-Amaah that my research works were good enough to be published in a book. His useful contributions have also enriched this book.

Special gratitude goes to Honourable F. K. Owusu-Adjapong, former Minister of Parliamentary Affairs and Majority Leader in Parliament, Ghana, and Past President of the Ghana Institution of Surveyors; Honourable Elizabeth Ohene, former Minister of Education, Ghana, and former Deputy Editor in the African Service of BBC World Service, London; and Joe Abbey, former Managing Director, TDC Development Company, Tema, Ghana, for their critical review of the original manuscript and valued technical contributions.

A very special word of appreciation also goes to my former colleagues – Jones Ofori-Boadu, Gifty Agbolosu, Sosthenes Dephor Galley, Samuel Tackey, Christiana Nyarko, Seth Owusu Boakye and Issifu Sedgah – at the Lands Commission, Ghana, for their invaluable inputs.

Preface

The contents of this book emerged from research works and presentations that I have delivered internationally and locally in combination with my rich experience as a Chartered Valuer and Chief Executive Officer in land administration in Ghana. Driven by passion, I deployed my skills, knowledge and experience to veer into a wide range of research in real estate market performance, finance and investment regardless of my job as a senior public servant. As an external examiner of the Kwame Nkrumah University of Science and Technology, I have kept pace with academia in teaching and learning about land economy and real estate at both the undergraduate and graduate levels. This unique opportunity has been capitalised to make this book achieve the combined effect of principles and practice.

Although small compared with advanced economies, there is a growing property stock in Ghana which constitutes the basis of an emergent real estate market. Much of the recently constructed stock is income-producing, and falls in the formal sector of the market where sale and leasing transactions are systematically recorded in the state land registry.

The aim of this book is to examine the real estate market in Ghana and its existing regulatory framework and provide a justification for its emergence in sub-Saharan Africa. It is intended to give an overview and also, more realistically, to concentrate on the nonexistent 'core' thematic areas of the market's development. I have considered the core areas to primarily consist of land administration, legal perspectives, market dynamics, investment potentials, market competitiveness, valuation and compensation.

The book would be useful for students, practitioners, real estate developers and investors. Professional advisors such as valuers, surveyors, lawyers, accountants, bankers, architects, planners and engineers would also find this book useful as an aid to their dealings in the real estate market. It brings together the professional and academic disciplines related to real estate development, management, finance and investment in an emerging economy. This information-packed referenced text provides readers with a good understanding of the main ingredients of the real estate market in the country and therefore of immediate benefit to professionals and their clients.

An important feature of this book is the way in which chapters are self-contained, and yet follow logically one from another. With this approach, readers can choose a reading path appropriate to their own specific needs without a loss of continuity.

Wilfred K. Anim-Odame, PhD,
MSc, BSc (Hons) FGhIS, MRICS
Accra, Ghana

Foreword

This book provides a unique account of the real estate market in Ghana, drawn from decades of first-hand experience that Dr. Wilfred K. Anim-Odame brings into light. In terms of his expertise, experience and zeal, I cannot think of a better-suited person to write this book. Wilfred has vitally contributed to the development of the real estate market in Ghana, not just through his achievement in the construction of the first-ever residential price and rent indices for the aggregate and disaggregate markets in the country. But also, his leadership role at the Ghana Lands Commission in building a solid and sustainable foundation for effective and efficient land services delivery. He has several published academic research works in the subject area and believes passionately in research-led interventions.

When reading the book, what stood out for me was the well-rounded coverage of the real estate market in the context of an emerging economy in Africa. While the book focuses on the real estate market in Ghana, it draws parallels with other emerging markets in sub-Saharan Africa that share several commonalities in land administration and real estate market development. At the same time, what is appealing is that the book delves into details on the interesting facets and peculiar forces driving the real estate market. For instance, the book devotes separate chapters to focus on the legal structures and legislations, covering in great detail the implementation of the long-term land administration reforms, while providing a unique perspective on the current and anticipated performance of the residential investment market.

With limited availability of high-quality data, lack of transparency, uncharacteristic valuation standards and complex legal structures governing the real estate markets in emerging economies, the book is the first to offer insightful and factual information on the workings and performance-drivers of the real estate market in Ghana. So, whether you are a student in real estate, land economy, surveying, planning, finance or law, an academic researcher in the built environment, a policymaker in land policy formulation or an industry practitioner interested in real estate investments in Africa, the book gives you some very original contributions and insights on real estate market characteristics, development and investment potentials.

In summary, what makes me recommend this book highly is that, firstly, it does an excellent job in making the readers appreciate the unique tenets of the real estate market in Ghana and in similar sub-Saharan African emerging economies, and secondly, the book is written by a real expert in the subject area.

Professor Dennis Philip
Professor in Finance
Director of Centre for Banking, Institutions and Development (CBID)
Department of Economics and Finance
Durham University Business School
Durham, United Kingdom

1 Introduction

1.1 Background

This book is a response to an information gap resulting from limited research in the real estate market in Ghana. It seeks to discover, examine and accentuate relevant information that remains essential to demystify the notion that the real estate market in Ghana is utterly opaque. Real estate market development is fundamentally shored up by a good land administration system that provides economic benefits for a modern cadastre. The benefits are not to only improve credit security and increase transparency of the market, but also to support its development.

Security of land tenure is an important land administration policy objective in most emerging economies, particularly in sub-Saharan Africa. However, this is difficult to achieve because of some failures in land administration systems. These include unclear land title, boundary disputes, counterclaims of ownership rights, institutional rigidities, overstaffing and corruption which tend to undermine public confidence. Ghana happens to be characterised by this type of land administration systems.

Security of land tenure is to be supported by clear legal title. It should also be widely seen as an important driver for real estate market development and economic development at large. However, the extent to which land registration alone is a sufficient condition for an efficient real estate market remains debatable.

The core contribution of this book is to explore the real estate market in Ghana and highlight its dynamics and decision-making variables based on the novel indices for the period 1992 to 2007. This will provide objective premise for further research and policy implementation. The processes which could be followed in other emerging markets with similar land registration systems are also emphasised.

The book in addition contains evidence of real estate market development in Ghana and its performance indicators. This work is also intended to promote the first- ever Ghanaian real estate indices that were developed from models that present a plausible account of trends over time. The performance indicators suggest investor returns in Ghana are consistent with the fundamental

Box 1.1 Ghana at a glance

National flag

Official name:	Republic of Ghana
Capital city:	Accra
Languages spoken:	English (official) and Twi, Ga, Ewe, Dagbani and many other local languages
Bordering countries:	Burkina Faso (north), Togo (East) and Cote d'Ivoire (West); Gulf of Guinea on the south
Population:	30.4 million (UN, 2019 estimate)
Size:	238,533 square kilometres
GDP:	US$ 66,984 million
GDP per capita:	US$ 2,212
Inflation rate:	11.2% (June 2020)
Currency:	Ghana Cedi (GH¢)
Exchange rates:	US$ 1.0 = GH¢5.67 UK Pound = GH¢7.00 Euro = GH¢6.36 (June 2020)
Key export commodities:	Gold, cocoa and oil
Dialing code:	+233
Internet domain:	.gh
International airport:	Kotoka (KIA) in Accra
Key business centres:	Accra, Kumasi, Koforidua, Sekondi-Takoradi, Tema, Cape Coast and Tamale
Standard business hours:	8:00 am–5:00 pm

theory of the behaviour of real estate markets and also in line with the results typically found in other emerging economies.

This book would be valuable to all those concerned with the evolution of and others who seek to understand the real estate market in Ghana – developers, investors, policy makers, students and the general public. The experience in other countries demonstrates that the production of real estate performance indicators such as those discussed in this book for the Ghanaian market can generate substantial revenues. Direct sales of information or licensing access to data generated are possible sources of revenue.

1.2 Brief country profile

Ghana is a West African country bounded by the Gulf of Guinea to the south, Cote d'Ivoire to the west, Burkina Faso to the north and Togo to the east. The country, which is similar in size to UK, has a population of 30.4 million

(UN, 2019 estimate), an equivalent to 0.39 percent of the world population. It was the first sub-Saharan colony to gain independence from Britain, on March 6, 1957. Political and economic instabilities between 1966 and 1991 were characterised by a series of military coups. Democratic reforms, and the enactment and adoption of the 1992 national Constitution have yielded stable, multiparty democratic governance to date. Ghana has traditionally depended on primary commodities such as cocoa, timber and gold as principal exports, with oil finds in 2008 (see Box 1.1 for additional information).

1.3 Motivation

This work is motivated by the view that real estate plays an important role in the development process for countries such as Ghana, and one that has received little attention in the literature on development economics, emerging market finance or international real estate investment markets. Real estate contributes to economic development in a number of ways.

First, a flexible and efficient supply of real estate is needed to support economic growth and attract inward investment in productive sectors. Second, in the capital markets, the expansion of real estate stock and the rise in its value form a major part of the accumulation of wealth associated with successful economic development. Third, those real estate values in turn represent a primary source of collateral for banks to lend to borrowers. Whether or not real estate market maturity plays an important role in the national economy, the development of mortgage markets is essential for sub-Saharan Africa economies. Mortgage markets will not only focus on the housing needs of the increasing population but also address the high unemployment rate through jobs creation in the construction and allied sectors.

Fourth, real estate is a major potential source of tax revenue for central and local governments, especially in sub-Saharan African countries where cash-based informal economies hamper the collection of other forms of taxation. For example, the total revenue from stamp duty in Ghana increased by 573 percent in 2000 to US$ 7,284,679 in 2007, an annualised increase of 31 percent per annum over the period, with 2019 revenue at US$ 21,347,740 (Land Valuation Board, 2008; Land Valuation Division, 2019). Also, local governments around the world such as the Metropolitan, Municipal and District Assemblies (MDAs) in Ghana depend greatly on property rates as an important revenue stream in their budgets. Fifth, as exemplified by the Asian crisis in the late 1990s, incorrectly priced and unstable real estate markets are major risk components for the banking and financial systems. The Asian crisis generated a large volume of evidence on the financial structure of real estate markets in those countries. Most countries in Southeast and East Asia recorded sustained and extremely high economic growth prior to the crisis, which translated into the real estate market. As foreign direct investment (FDI) increased, the economy grew and the demand for high quality real estate also increased. The situation triggered off a rise in property values and a scale-up of new development supported by bank lending. Mera and Renaud

(2000) finds bank exposure to real estate loans as high as 20 percent to 50 percent in these countries. The combined effect of the overexposure of banks to real estate and the subsequent collapse of the real estate markets exposed the countries in the subregion to economic and financial crises.

1.4 Real estate market performance

Residential real estate constitutes the largest segment of the market in Ghana. The nascent residential market provides for either owner occupation or investment vehicles for rental income. Residential submarkets for investment purposes are typically apartments, townhouses, single-family homes and gated communities. Owner-occupied properties are, in contrast, detached houses or in some cases shared accommodation with tenants.

The rented residential market accounts for 31 percent of all households (Ghana Statistical Service, 2010). Pricing of a residential property as expected, is demand- and supply-driven. Population growth, formation of new households and levels of income in the long run will influence the demand. Supply factors include availability of capital and planning regulations. It is anticipated that over time, there will be a pattern of residential investment to match demand.

The absence of a robust mortgage market in Ghana is a restraining force in the development of the residential market. In effect, Ghana, like most emerging economies, lags far behind developed economies in terms of availability of real estate finance. Requirements for a mortgage transaction vary from one financial institution to the other, and also depend on the quantum of the loan as well as whether the security offered is owner-occupied, single-let, multi-let or a portfolio of properties. Financial institutions require some basic documentations to conclude a mortgage transaction. Specific quantitative requirements include a recent valuation on the property to estimate the loan to value ratio, interest cover ratio and residual loan ratio. Mortgagees (lenders) also appraise the track record of mortgagors (borrowers) to establish potential default risk. Banks have held strongly to the principle of considering a 'good story' from every potential borrower on an account that each property is certainly unique.

The most systematic and extensive classification of real estate markets by indicators of data transparency and other measures of 'maturity' can be found in the 'Global Real Estate Transparency Index (GRETI)' produced by Jones Lang LaSalle Incorporated (JLL). In the past two decades, JLL has tracked real estate transparency and championed higher standards in several economies. The 10th edition of GRETI was produced in 2018 with an increased coverage from 37 to 100 countries and extended scope to quantify 186 separate elements of transparency.

The construction of real estate performance indices covers factors that are considered important by global real estate investors. The Global Transparency Index (GTI) is a weighted score of subjective ratings covering six thematic areas – performance measurement, market fundamentals, governance of listed vehicles, regulatory and legal, transaction process and sustainability. Only 14 sub-Saharan African countries were covered in the 2018 edition, with South Africa (best performer in Africa) and Ghana ranked 21st and 76th, respectively. Nigeria and Rwanda ranked 67th and 78th, respectively, and together with Ghana were classified as low transparent markets; South Africa was pegged in the transparent category. Countries such as UK, Australia, US, France, Canada, Netherlands, New Zealand, Germany, Ireland and Sweden with developed real estate markets featured high in the rankings. On the city level, London leads the rankings as the world's most transparent real estate market. It confirms its role as the favoured destination for global capital. Other cities such as Los Angeles, Sydney, San Francisco and New York are featured in the Top 5 as highly transparent.

1.5 Existing works on real estate markets in emerging economies

Despite their importance, real estate markets in emerging economies, particularly in sub-Saharan Africa, have received surprisingly little attention in research literature. In Ghana specifically, very small existing literature has focused primarily on the description of formal versus informal real estate market mechanisms with limited quantitative analysis on market performance and investment potentials.

Elsewhere, a rise in cross-border flows of real estate investment has occurred as well as an even more dramatic increase in the flow of real estate capital from advanced countries into Asia and the transition economies of Central and Eastern Europe. This globalisation of real estate investment has been accompanied by a growth in research on the real estate markets of emerging and transition economies, from both academic and industry sources. Firms of real estate intermediaries have also expanded the coverage of the standard market indicators to include rental growth, capital growth, price and rental indices, yields, total returns and market stock in mature real estate markets.

As with research on emerging equity markets, much of the work on these emerging real estate markets from academic and industry sources takes the viewpoint of investors from the advanced economies. It focuses on questions like the ability of new markets to meet the standards of professionalism and transparency required by inward investors, for example, McGreal *et al.*, (2001) on Central and Eastern Europe, and Jones Lang LaSalle (2008) on measures of transparency or on the portfolio benefits of international diversification; for a general review, see Sirmans and Worzala (2003).

Seek (1995) defines one of the earliest characterisations of real estate market maturity for emerging countries based on the strength and structure of the economy, foreign investment levels and controls, market size and quality of infrastructure. In Southeast Asia, real estate market evolution has been a function of city growth or urbanisation, emergence of the investment market and a profound shift in principal areas of the national economy. On these typologies, in the mid-1990s, Singapore was rated as the only advanced real estate market in the region. In Thailand, the Bangkok prime office market was, for example, characterised by a dominance of family-controlled business organisations

(Armitage, 1996), reinforced by a prohibition of real estate ownership-control by 'aliens' and severely affected by restrictions on repatriation of profits.

Keith *et al.*, (2000) in a study of Central and Eastern European countries points out that the development of real estate markets has been constrained by a wide range of factors including the lack of adequate legal framework and the lack of stable banking and financial services systems. These institutional constraints meant that transitional economies have less developed real estate markets than market economies with comparable per capita incomes. Others such as the Polish real estate market have been hampered by insufficient legal documentation and weak real estate professional advisory services, and characterised by difficult access to land and mortgage registers (Belniak and Schwartz, 2000).

Real estate markets in emerging economies are generally characterised by poorly developed systems of data collection, access and dissemination. Adair *et al.*, (2004) summarises that data transparency is a key characteristic of a mature market, and markets that are able to demonstrate that they possess such data have a competitive advantage and are more likely to attract private sector investment funds.

For these reasons, most African countries lack active real estate investment markets. To a large extent, the primary sources of market evidence, which shape real estate research in advanced economies and in a growing list of transitional economies, are limited in sub-Saharan Africa. The construction of real estate indices requires a substantial base of professional investors, who will conduct full open-market valuations of their assets to international standards at least once a year. It is unlikely that these conditions can currently be met in most sub-Sahara African countries outside South Africa. Any efforts to create measures of market performance will probably require the alternative methodology based on real estate transactions data.

Outside of South Africa, published research on sub-Saharan African real estate markets has concentrated mainly on institutional structures and constraints on market development. One substantial body of works deals with land tenure and ownership rights, often suggesting that traditional forms of land ownership constrain real estate development and investment (see Kasanga and Kotey, 2001; Abdulai and Owusu-Ansah, 2014; Antwi and Adams, 2003 for Ghana; O'Connor, 1983; Omirin, 1994, 1998, 1999 for Nigeria; Okoth-Ogendo, 1982; Migot-Adholla *et al.*, 1994 for Kenya). A second strand of work deals with the scale and consequences of governmental intervention in land markets (see Asiama, 1990; Antwi, 1995; Kasanga *et al.*, 1996; Adams *et al.*, 1996; Quan, 1997; Asabere, 2007). These studies arrive at similar general conclusions, that such interventions have often taken the form of policies which are either skewed towards a small segment of the society or produced investment disincentives. A third body of research concentrates on the technical requirements for laying the foundations for efficient real estate data recording and housing finance (see Fiadzo, 2004; CHF International, 2004; Mahama, 2006; Buckley and Mathema, 2007; Owusu-Ansah *et al.*, 2018; Owusu-Ansah *et al.*, 2020; Teye *et al.*, 2015; Owusu-Manu *et al.*, 2018; Donkor-Hyiaman and Ghartey, 2017). These studies recommend a common agenda to address the fundamentals, provide reliable database to support robust empirical analysis of the real estate market and develop the housing finance in Ghana.

The small number of studies specific to Ghana which deal with the estimation of real estate values and returns are of the most direct relevance to the primary objective of this book. The earliest work of this type is Asabere (1981). It applies hedonic analysis to explain the sale price of vacant lands in Accra using limited data of only 211 transactions. It reveals land value determinants in the formal sector to include location, land tenure, lot size and site services. The results also suggest that lands held by traditional authorities were sold at discount prices. Antwi (2002) targets the informal real estate market and investigates the relationship between price of building plots and explanatory variables including neighbourhood quality, state land, customary land, finance, market information and registration cost. The study applies hedonic methods to a small sample size of 305 transaction-based data to show that real estate titling and tenure are not significant factors in price determination; purchasers are perceived to be buying perpetual rights. As in Asabere (1981), no time series estimates of prices were produced.

Time series to generate measures of change in residential values by Antwi and Omirin (2006) were rather limited to primary data on rental values and lease premiums for Accra, Ghana, and Lagos, Nigeria, for 1999 to 2003. The study estimates real annual capital growth at 10 percent per annum in the formal residential market in Accra, with an average rental yield estimated at 6 percent. It also suggests that yields and performance in the formal and informal sectors are broadly comparable. Owusu-Ansah *et al.*, (2017) investigates real estate prices in Ghana, but that is also restricted to showing that temporal aggregation may not be a serious issue for developing markets due to data limitations. Similarly, Soyeh *et al.*, (2020) analyses the real estate market by showing the impact of gated developments on property values and rents in Accra, Ghana.

Both information sources and published literature on African real estate markets are, on the whole, limited. With the partial exception of South Africa, there are few sources, and, for instance, no long time series of the market indicators of prices, rents, yields, nominal and real returns which are the primary data used to track conditions in mature markets. Again, the South African real estate markets share characteristics of mature markets in terms of data quality and transparency, valuation standards and the active participation of international market intermediaries. Given the lack of primary data, published research on sub-Saharan African real estate markets has consisted mainly of studies which are narrow in scope, which this book seeks to explore as a substantial contribution to the literature.

1.6 Objective of the book

Against this background, the author seeks to achieve the objective of providing an understanding of the fundamentals and dynamics of the real estate market in Ghana. This is the first book on the real estate market in Ghana that addresses the full range of topics covered here. Readers such as undergraduate and graduate students in land economy, real estate, estate management and business studies in sub-Saharan Africa will find this book a valuable textbook. Additionally, the book will serve as a practical resource for investors, professionals and other readers to understand the dynamics of the real estate markets in Ghana and selected countries with similar land administration systems in the subregion. Such systems, originally based on British practices, exist in countries such as Ghana, Nigeria, Kenya, Uganda and Tanzania.

1.7 Structure of the book

The remainder of this book is divided into six chapters. Chapter 2 covers land administration systems in Ghana and highlights the basics, policies, strategic interventions, outcomes and the path ahead in achieving efficiency and effectiveness. In Chapter 3, the legal framework for real estate transactions and market development is treated. Chapter 4 examines the market dynamics. It provides market performance indicators at both aggregate and disaggregate levels. Chapters 5 focuses on the investment potentials and provides empirical benchmarks intended to inform investors in decision-making. The penultimate chapter highlights the competitiveness of the real estate market in Ghana. First, it compares real estate with other asset classes in the economy. Second, it appraises the real estate market against selected peers in sub-Saharan Africa to make a case for Ghana as a real estate investment destination. Third, variation in returns across submarkets, and the linkages between investment performance and the wider economy, are analysed. Chapter 7 elucidates the principles underlining the traditional methods of real estate valuation. It assesses the quality of infrastructure and provides guidelines to build capacity and competences in real estate valuation. Compensation for expropriated property is also treated within rural and urban context.

References

Abdulai, R. and Owusu-Ansah, A. (2014). Land information management and landed property ownership security: Evidence from state-sponsored court system. *Habitat International*, 42, pp. 131–137.

Adair, A., Allen, S., Berry, J. and McGreal, S. (2004). *The development of land and property markets in Central and Eastern Europe: Issues of data*. London: RICS Foundation, September.

Adams, M., Cassidy, E., Cusworth, J., Lowcock, M. and Tempest, F. (1996). *ODA land appraisal mission to Zimbabwe*. London: British Development Division in Central Africa.

Anim-Odame, W. (2009). *Residential real estate investment in emerging economies: The case of Ghana*. Unpublished PhD Thesis, Cass Business School, Faculty of Finance, City University, London.

Anim-Odame, W. (2012). The nascent real estate market in Ghana. *Journal of Real Estate Literature*, 20 (2), pp. 289–304.

Anim-Odame, W. (2013). *Real estate investment market in Africa: The case of Ghana.* 13th Annual Conference of the African Real Estate Society, Kigali, Rwanda, October 23–26.

Anim-Odame, W. (2016). Developing real estate markets in sub-Sahara Africa: The fundamentals. *Real Estate Finance*, 32 (1), Summer, pp. 26–32.

Anim-Odame, W., Key, K. and Stevenson, S. (2009). Measures of real estate values from land registration and valuation systems in emerging economies: The case of Ghana. *Journal of Real Estate Literature*, 17 (1), pp. 63–84.

Anim-Odame, W., Key, T. and Stevenson, S. (2010a). The Ghanaian transaction-based residential indices. *International Journal for Housing Market and Analysis*, 3 (3), pp. 216–232. 9th Annual Conference of the African Real Estate Society, Lagos, Nigeria; October 20–22, 2009.

Anim-Odame, W., Key, T. and Stevenson, S. (2010b). Residential market development in sub-Saharan Africa. *International Journal for Housing Market and Analysis*, 3 (4), pp. 308–326.

Antwi, A. (1995). *An economic perspective of land policy implementation in developing economies: The case of Accra, Ghana.* London: Our Common Estate Series, RICS.

Antwi, A. (2002). *A study of informal urban land transactions in Accra, Ghana.* London: Our Common Estate, RICS.

Antwi, A. and Adams, J. (2003). Economic rationality and informal urban land transactions in Accra, Ghana. *Journal of Real Estate Research*, 20 (1), pp. 67–90.

Antwi, A. and Omirin, M. (2006). The investment performance of informal properties in Accra, Ghana and Lagos, Nigeria. *RICS Research Paper Series*, 6 (4).

Armitage, L. (1996). *Constraints to the operation of commercial real estate market in South-East Asia.* London: RICS Research Conference, The Cutting Edge.

Asabere, P. (1981). The determinants of land values in an African city: The case of Accra, Ghana. *Land Economics*, 57 (3), pp. 385–397.

Asabere, P. (2007). The demise of the rent-controlled public housing programmes of Ghana: The story of the Tema Development Corporation. *Urban Studies*, 44 (10), pp. 1919–1935.

Asiama, S. (1990). Land for housing the urban poor in Africa: Some policy options. In: P. Amis and P. Lloyd, ed., *Housing Africa's urban poor.* 1st ed. Manchester: Manchester University Press, pp. 239–251.

Belniak, S. and Schwartz Jr., A. (2000). The nascent Polish real estate market. *Journal of Real Estate Literature*, 8 (1), pp. 19–33.

Buckley, R. and Mathema, A. (2007). *Is Accra a superstar city?* Washington, DC: The World Bank, Policy Research Working Paper.

CHF International. (2004). *Strategic assessment of the affordable housing sector in Ghana.* Silver Spring: CHF International.

Donkor-Hyiaman, K. and Ghartey, K. (2017). Legal origins and mortgage finance contradictions. *International Journal of Housing Markets and Analysis*, 10 (1), pp. 156–179.

Fiadzo, E. (2004). *Estimating the determinants of housing quality: The case of Ghana.* Cambridge: Joint Centre for Housing Studies of Harvard University, Working Paper Series W04–6.

Ghana Statistical Service. (2010). *Population and housing census data analysis report.* Accra: Ghana Statistical Service.

Jones Lang LaSalle. (2008). Global real estate transparency index. *Global Research.*

Kasanga, R., Cochrane, J., King, R. and Roth, M. (1996). *Land markets and legal contradictions in the peri-urban area of Accra, Ghana: Informal interviews and secondary data investigations.* Madison, WI: Land Tenure Centre, pp. 1–90, Research Paper.

Kasanga, R. and Kotey, N. (2001). *Land management in Ghana: Building on traditional and modernity.* London: Department for International Development (DFID).

Keith, S., Heywood, M., Adlington, G., Perrotta, L. and Munro-Faure, P. (2000). *Developing real estate markets in transition economies*. Background Paper for Special Session 1 on Mobilising Financial Resources for Transformation and Development – The Domestic Dimension, UN/ECE Secretariat.

Land Valuation Board. (2008). Annual Report, Accra, Ghana.

Land Valuation Division. (2019). Annual Report, Accra, Ghana.

Mahama, C. (2006). Acquisition and affordability of land for housing in urban Ghana: A study in the formal land market dynamics. *RICS Research Paper Series*, 6 (10).

McGreal, S., Parsa, A. and Keivani, R. (2001). Perceptions of real estate markets in central Europe: A survey of European investors. *Journal of Real Estate Literature*, 9 (2), pp. 145–159.

Mera, K. and Renaud, B. (2000). *Asia's financial crisis and the role of real estate*. New York: M. E. Sharpe Inc.

Migot-Adholla, S., Benneh, G., Place, F. and Atsu, S. (1994). Land, security of tenure, and productivity in Ghana. In: J. Bruce and S. Migot-Adholla ed., *Searching for land tenure security in Africa*. 1st ed. Iowa: Kendall/Hunt Publishing Company, pp. 97–114.

O'Connor, A. (1983). *The African city*. Essex: The Anchor Press Ltd, pp. 25–30.

Okoth-Ogendo, H. (1982). *The perils of land tenure reform*. Workshop on Land Policy and Agricultural Production in Eastern and Southern Africa Countries. Gaborone, Botswana.

Omirin, M. (1994). *Land affordability for private low-income housing in Lagos metropolitan area*. Technical Research Paper No.1, Faculty of Environmental Sciences, University of Lagos, Nigeria.

Omirin, M. (1998). Land accessibility and low-income house building activity in Lagos metropolitan area. *Journal of Environmental Studies*, 1 (1), pp. 76–91.

Omirin, M. (1999). Land tenure systems versus housing builders' requirements for security – The Lagos experience. *Journal of Environmental Studies*, 2 (1), pp. 42–53.

Owusu-Ansah, A., Adolwine, W. and Yeboah, E. (2017). Construction of real estate price indices for developing housing markets: Does temporal aggregation matter? *International Journal of Housing Markets and Analysis*, 10 (3), pp. 371–383.

Owusu-Ansah, A., Anim-Odame, W. and Azasu, S. (2020). Examination of the dynamics of house prices in urban Ghana. *African Geographical Review*. DOI: 10.1080/19376812.2020.1761844.

Owusu-Ansah, A., Ohemeng-Mensah, D., Abdulai, R. and Obeng-Odoom, F. (2018). Public choice theory and rental housing: An examination of rental housing contracts in Ghana. *Housing Studies*, 33 (6), pp. 938–959.

Owusu-Manu, D., Edwards, D., Parn, E., Asiedu, R. and Aboagye, A. (2018). Determinants of mortgage price affordability: A study of Ghana. *International Journal of Housing Markets and Analysis*, 11 (4), pp. 734–751.

Quan, J. (1997). *The importance of land tenure to poverty eradication and sustainable development in sub-Saharan Africa*. Background report for the 1997 UK Government White Paper on International Development, July, DFID, London.

Seek, N. (1995). *Institutional participation in Asia-Pacific real estate markets: Are the benefits worth the risks?* Proceedings of the Pacific Rim Council on Urban Development Conference, Brisbane, Australia.

Sirmans, C. and Worzala, E. (2003). International direct real estate investment: A review of the literature. *Urban Studies*, 40, pp. 108–114.

Soyeh, K., Asabere, P. and Owusu-Ansah, A. (2020). Price and rental differentials in gated versus non-gated communities: The case of Accra, Ghana. *Housing Studies*. DOI: 10.1080/02673037.2020.1789566.

Teye, J., Teye, I. and Asiedu, M. (2015). Financing housing in Ghana: Challenges to the development of formal mortgage system. *Journal of Housing and the Built Environment*, 30, pp. 1–16.

United Nations, Department of Economic and Social Affairs, Population Division. (2019). *World population prospects, volume 1: Comprehensive tables* (ST/ESA/SER.A/426). New York: United Nations, p. 24.

2 Land administration

2.1 Background

Land in its physical form of buildings and resources is characterised by cognitive concepts that reflect the different ways people think about it worldwide. These concepts, which include the following, are diversified and ever-changing.

Land as nature

Land comprises all naturally occurring resources whose supply is fixed. It provides features of the working of nature without human efforts and exists within the envelope of nature and also as the natural environment.

Land as a resource

Land is a source of wealth creation for an individual, family or corporate entity. It is also a reliable source of revenue for central and local governments. The source of power or status of an individual, family, community or nation can be traced to their or its land mass and composition. Land can be let or sold to raise capital and is usually a preferred collateral due to its long-term characteristic.

Land as a factor of production

Land is the primary factor of production in economics, besides labour, capital and entrepreneurship. It is generally described as that part of nature that includes farmlands, forests, minerals, rivers and the sky. Sometimes, land is considered as more than the mere surface of the earth. Anything that is or becomes affixed to the land becomes part of it as in the Latin principle of *quicquid plantatur solo, solo cedit*, which literally means 'whatever is affixed to the soil belongs to the soil.'

Land as a commodity

Land can be traded in the real estate market, with spatial land use as a tool to promote its trading as a residential, commercial, industrial, farming or recreational commodity in a disaggregate market. As with other commodities, its price is demand- and supply-driven.

Land as a physical space

Land provides a fixed space for life. Take away land, and there is no life. Even after life, all living creatures return to land. It thus defines the surface of the earth and provides space for the built environment, water bodies, mountains, valleys and other natural physical features.

Land as a deity

Some societies, particularly in sub-Saharan Africa, treat land as the source of their life and sustenance. Land is considered as the abode of ancestral spirits that exercise control over the people who use it. Sometimes land is perceived as a communal asset. Ollennu (1962) puts it lyrically that land belongs to a vast family, of which many are dead, a few are living, and countless hosts are still unborn. Accordingly, the values and spiritual association with land by the Akans in Ghana make them highly unwilling to give up land. The Akan[1] proverb *'tumi nyinaa wo asaase so,'* which literally means 'all power is in the land,' is an acknowledgement that land is a deity.

Land as a community

Land is a location that denotes homeland, motherland or fatherland. It symbolises a group of people living in a particular community with a common interest and of a given name of identification. In Ghana, stool[2] and family lands are held in trust for the larger group or community.

Land as a human right

The Universal Declaration of Human Rights articulates fundamental rights and freedoms for all to include the right to own property. Article 17 provides that everyone has the right to own property (United Nations, 1948). This is enunciated by Article 36 (7) of the 1992 Constitution of the Republic of Ghana where the state guarantees the ownership of property and the right of inheritance.

2.2 Land administration systems

Land administration entails the processes of recording and disseminating information on land ownership, value and use. These three facets of land administration are inextricably linked and cover the processes and systems of managing the allotment of land rights; valuation and taxation; surveying and mapping of land; and control of land use. The processes of recording and dissemination are the traditional functions of land sector agencies responsible for surveying and mapping, land management and registration, land valuation, and land use and spatial planning.

First, these processes address parcel delineation by defining the land for which an interest is granted, demarcate boundaries on the ground and translate these boundaries into writing, numerically and graphically. Second, they record and guarantee information on land ownership through a series of processes that are concerned with establishing the root of titles. This process is essential to provide a credible foundation for the acquisition, enjoyment and disposal of interests and rights in land. It also ensures tenure security. It encompasses property conveyancing, including decisions on transfers, subdivisions, mortgages and land use policies in consultation with appropriate agencies. Third, the processes extend to the economic utility of land. Valuation of land provides the basis of wealth accumulation and also supports the mobilisation of local and central government revenue. Valuation further serves as an incentive to consolidate or reallocate land or use land for a specific purpose. Fourth, all human activities must manifest in space and require land allocation to achieve its highest and best use. Land use restrictions that are imposed through zoning mechanisms are intended to designate parcels of land for specific purposes such as residential, commercial, industrial, agricultural and recreational. Land use and spatial planning has therefore become a central prerequisite for spatial development. In some jurisdictions, separate agencies are established to perform these functions. But there is a potential danger for duplication of functions and resources among these agencies. In Ghana, there are three agencies – the Lands Commission for surveying and mapping, land management and registration, and land valuation; the Office of the Administrator of Stool Lands for stool lands revenue mobilisation and disbursement; and the Land Use and Spatial Planning Authority for land use and spatial planning.

Land administration is capital-intensive and -expensive. A modern land administration system should be characterised by a credible and accessible cadastre for each of the attributes – ownership, value and use. A land cadastre that is based on a proprietary plan with particulars on ownership, values, taxation and use can be distinguished from a land register, which covers only ownership particulars. A land cadastre is therefore of great importance in national development. For example, in Sweden and Finland, cadastres are established to cover land consolidation, ownership rights, valuation, taxation, registration and cadastral mapping. A good land administration system will produce several benefits including the following.

Repository of credible data

Data on land ownership, value and uses are to be carefully held and managed by professionals. Data credibility and accessibility are the basic requirements for real estate market research, and the bedrock for policy formulation. It is possible to extract transaction-based data from such a database to construct indices and generate other performance indicators to promote the market development. Current and historical data will make property related taxation – stamp duty, capital gains tax, gift tax, rental income tax – efficient and transparent.

Safeguard state and vested lands

State and vested lands are held for specific purposes and must be protected. Clear and harmonised records on the location, plot size, intended use, particulars of original owners, quantum of compensation paid or outstanding and details of Executive Instruments can be made accessible. The records will provide certainty and prevent adverse claims on those lands.

Functional mortgage market

The mortgage market thrives on credible and accessible real estate market indicators such as vacancy rate, yield, rent and price indices. A good land cadastre that provides title details and assures guaranteed title could support the mortgage market. Usually mortgage transactions are recorded as a thematic layer in the cadastre to serve as an encumbrance on the subject property, a further guarantee in favour of the mortgagee.

Security of title

Land is a long-term asset that requires a secure title. Title duly registered and captured in the cadastre provides rights that are enforceable. Such rights can easily be verified from the cadastre and authenticated by a public officer as a proof in evidence. The information in the cadastre should be open for public access at a reasonable cost to allow for third party rights identification. Also, it should serve as a notice to the whole world.

Reduced land disputes

Indeterminate land boundaries are recipes for litigation but a good land administration system should provide a nationwide land cadastre. This will deliver certainty of ownership with minimal boundary overlaps, conflicting claims and disputes.

Sustainable management of the environment

Security of tenure is key for sustainable planning and management of the environment. A land cadastre provides a platform to record conservation areas and generate information on locations of sites of historical, cultural and scientific interest. It also facilitates the preparation of environmental impact assessment reports.

Planning and infrastructure development

A good land cadastre must permit smooth integration with other developmental systems to support planning and development. Planning for infrastructural development depends on the availability of spatial data and cadastral plans.

Facilitate land reform and market development

A classification of land rights that is comprehensive, accurate and up-to-date can easily be established from the cadastre to inform policy. Also, a good culture of quality, professional service and client satisfaction can be achieved to develop the land market.

2.3 Antecedents to current land administration systems

As with many other emerging economies, the land registration systems in Ghana have experienced a long history. Woodman (1988) and Agbosu (1990) claim land registration in Ghana was first introduced in 1883 with the Land Registration Ordinance, followed by the Land Registry Ordinance in 1895. Though these statutes form the distant antecedents to the current systems, they were created by the colonial administration mainly to protect land rights of minority white merchants. Even in the coastal areas where colonial interests in the land market were at that time most developed, plural tenures under which systems of common law enacted by legislation and customary law continued to coexist (Woodman, 1988). Problems such as inadequate security of tenure, indeterminate allodial boundaries, disputes and litigation, and difficult access to land and general indiscipline in the land market could be the products of the duality system – customary and common law.

A multiplicity of laws was enacted by pre- and post-independence governments to deal with specific land-related problems on an ad hoc basis, not forming part of a comprehensive policy on land administration. Some of these statues include the Public Lands Ordinance, 1876 (Cap 134); Land Appropriation Ordinance, 1901; Land and Native Rights Ordinance, 1927 (Cap 143); Kumasi Lands Ordinance, 1943 (Cap 145); Akim Abuakwa (Stool Revenue) Act (No. 28), 1958; and Stool Lands Act, 1960 (Act 27).

The Land Registry Act, 1962 (Act 122), though with nationwide coverage, recorded only formal transaction deeds like its predecessors and did not register proprietary interests established under customary claims. The Land Title Registration Act, 1986 (PNDCL, 152) for the first time provided for systematic registration of all interests in land under both common law and customary ownerships in the country. By the late 1990s, however, the progress of registration was still being limited to only the Greater Accra Region, comprising major cities such as Accra and Tema and part of Kumasi, the regional capital of the Ashanti Region. Though within those areas the law prescribed systematic registration, its implementation remained patchy. The transition from Act 122 to PNDCL 152 appeared not to have been properly managed. Institutional bottlenecks such as lack of cooperation between the Lands Commission and the then Land Title Registry as the agencies involved in the process, lack of capacity and resources and the reliance on numerous, overlapping and outdated statutes accounted for that situation.

In all the indigenous social administrations, land is communally held in trust for the tribe, clan or family, and administered by the chiefs, *tendambas*[3] or heads of these sociopolitical entities. Members of these entities or 'indigenes' have had guaranteed access to their land. Nevertheless, as the population increased and put pressure on land, indigenous arrangements under which individual members of the lineage enjoyed general rights of access to land have been rendered untenable. Commercial transactions in land and the transformation of inheritance principles compounded by increasing pressure and demand have given rise to increased litigation over land. Some indigenes have sought to undermine the authority of their chiefs or heads of families and gone ahead to conclude land transactions without the knowledge and consent of the chiefs or heads, resulting in disputes. The need for a coherent land policy and effective land administration in the long-term informed the government in 1999 to develop the first-ever national land policy.

2.4 The National Land Policy

The Government of Ghana introduced its comprehensive National Land Policy in June 1999 with a long-term goal. The policy seeks to stimulate economic development, reduce poverty and promote social stability by improving security of land tenure, simplifying the process for accessing land, and making it fair, transparent and efficient. Further, it aims at developing the land market and fostering prudent land management. The policy addresses challenges of the land sector including inadequate policy and legal framework, fragmented institutional arrangements and weak capacity, weak land administration systems, underdeveloped land registration system, inefficient land markets, and compulsory acquisitions of land by government without compensation (Ministry of Lands and Forestry, 1999).

The long-term goal of the policy was to be achieved through the implementation of a 15–25-year land administration reform dubbed the Land Administration Project (LAP), largely funded by development partners with the World Bank as the lead partner. The first phase sought to address the weak fundamentals and lay long-term foundation with the focus on the following.

Inadequate policy and legal framework

Land as an asset class provides the foundation for economic activities and the functioning of markets, and governments at both central and local level. Norms and regulations, together with systems, are thus developed to control and legally protect the rights and interest held in land to address land market imperfections.

Land administration in Ghana is characterised by the duality of customary and common law as well as court judgements that have been ruled on customary subjects and resulted in a body of legal precedents. Prior to the commencement of LAP, it was reported that 166 laws existed to either regulate land administration or establish mandates of different land sector agencies or both. Many of the laws were not only outdated but also conflicted with one another. There was a high incidence of reliance on these laws to prolong land litigation in the courts and in some cases confuse issues. One of the key performance indicators for phase one of LAP was thus to reduce the estimated 35,000 land cases in courts; the Greater Accra Region alone was reported to have over 15,000 land disputes, mainly due to boundary overlaps or conflicting claims of ownership pending in the courts as of July 2003.

Several agencies existed to administer public, vested and stool lands (Lands Commission); settle stool land boundary disputes (Stool Land Boundary Commission); collect and disburse stool land revenue (Office of the Administrator of Stool Lands); determine land and property values for various purposes, rateable values and compensation for public land acquisition (Land Valuation Board); undertake national land survey and mapping, licensing of land surveyors and verification of survey plans (Survey Department); and registration of titles and protection of interest in land (Land Title Registry). The multiplicity of land sector agencies resulted in the duplication of functions and resources, unproductive competition between agency heads and even among technical staff and protection of turfs. Turnaround time for land services delivery and transaction costs had been very high due to institutional inefficiency.

Conflicts of interest between and within land-owning groups and even the state give rise to tenure insecurity. Lives of parties involved in litigation and their properties are sometimes in danger. The situation is worsened by the slow determination of land cases in court, which adds up to the costs of transactions in the real estate market. In Ghana, as with other sub-Saharan African countries, tenure insecurity means that large parts of the population are unable to realise the full benefits of land ownership. Among which are access to credit, sustainable management of resources, and investment incentives and ability to alienate. Large tracts of land have been compulsorily acquired by the government, and have not been fully utilised and/or often with unpaid compensation. This situation has truncated the sources of livelihood of the land owners, and led to unnecessary tension between original landowners and the state. Phase one of LAP was therefore designed to harmonise land policies and the legislative framework with customary law for sustainable land administration.

Undeveloped land registration system and inefficient land market

Security of land ownership is certainly enhanced by identifying and protecting property rights and interests. This can be achieved through an efficient and effective land registration system. The proposition of land title registration is to give certainty and facilitate proof of title. Other characteristics are to render dealings in land safe, simple and cheap and prevent transaction frauds. With the exception of few cities and towns in the country that have benefited from urban redevelopment projects, there is no systematic cadastral mapping, registration and land titling program.

Allodial lands held by stools, skins and families are largely characterised by indeterminate boundaries due to lack of reliable maps and plans. Outdated and inaccurate boundary plans are relied upon and the consequences are protracted litigation and freezing of land for developments. Frequent encroachments on undeveloped lands, multiple transactions and unapproved development schemes resulting in haphazard developments, environmental degradation and frequent violent confrontations between and among conflicting claimants are also rife. Haphazard developments, overdominance of residential in relation to other land uses such as schools, leisure and open spaces, restricted accessibility and poor drainage systems are common features of the built environment.

The increasing demand for urban land relative to its fixed supply underpins the land market inefficiencies. There is a gross demand and supply mismatch for residential purposes that has resulted in highly priced urban lands and haphazardly developed peri-urban lands. This situation is often not supported by requisite infrastructure such as access roads, drains, electricity and pipe-borne water.

In terms of financing, there is usually a great loss of revenue to the central and local governments because most of the land transactions in the cities and towns are informal and unregistered. Funding for social, environmental and infrastructural development continues to be the sole burden of the central government and Metropolitan, Municipal and District Assemblies. An obvious response was to customise LAP to establish an efficient, fair and transparent system of land titling, registration, land use planning and valuation in the country to address the weaknesses.

Fragmented institutional arrangements and weak capacity

A good land governance promotes tenure security and national development. Across the West African subregion, there are weak governance structures for both public and customary lands, resulting in weak and inefficient institutions. A large stock of lands in Ghana, estimated at 80 percent, are communally owned and held either by a stool, skin or family in trust for the larger community or group. Whilst stool lands are a common feature of land ownership in the Akan traditional areas in the middle and southern parts of the country, northern Ghana is differentiated by skin lands. The 1992 Constitution reinforces traditional land ownership. Article 267 (1) of the Constitution provides that 'all stool lands in Ghana shall vest in the appropriate stool on behalf of, and in trust of the subjects of the stool in accordance with customary law and usage.' The family land holding category represents a private communal land ownership prevalent in some regions including Volta, Greater Accra, Central, Eastern and Oti. The 20 percent residue is either state or vested land together with all water bodies in the country. State lands are compulsorily acquired by the president of the Republic of Ghana for public purposes or in the public interest. Sandwiched between state and stool lands is a small percentage of vested lands with a split of holding rights between the state as the managers and allodial owners as beneficiaries of the revenue.

Six land sector agencies – the Land Valuation Board, Lands Commission, Survey Department, Land Title Registry, Office of the Administrator of Stool Lands and Town and Country Planning Department – existed with fragmented and sometimes overlapping responsibilities prior to 2008. Each agency performed an aspect of land administration such as valuation; deed registration and management of public, stool and vested lands; stool land revenue mobilisation and disbursement; title registration; surveying and mapping; and land use planning with limited collaboration. Lengthy and cumbersome procedures for land acquisition as well as the high cost of land transactions and registration culminated in rent seeking behaviour among staff of the agencies. Duplication of functions and resources among the agencies and unproductive competition were the other weaknesses that informed the decision to undertake institutional reform and capacity building under LAP.

2.5 Specific land administration project interventions

The Land Administration Project[4] phase one (LAP 1), which started on October 13, 2003, was envisioned to lay the foundation for implementation of the long-term land administration reform. Its main objective was to develop a sustainable and well-functioning land administration system that was fair, efficient, cost effective and decentralised and that enhanced land tenure security through five interventions. First, harmonise land policies and the legislative framework with customary law for sustainable land administration. Second, undertake institutional reform and capacity building for comprehensive improvement in the land administration system. Third, establish an efficient, fair and transparent system of land titling, registration and valuation. Fourth, develop community-level land dispute resolution mechanisms. Fifth, issue and register land titles in selected pilot urban and rural areas.

LAP 1 had four components to provide an enabling environment for exploration, testing and learning by doing (World Bank, 2003). The components and subcomponents were:

1 Harmonising land policy and regulatory framework for sustainable land administration.

   a Revisions of policies, laws and regulations for an effective and efficient land administration.
   b Strengthening of civil courts to expedite resolution of land cases and developing alternative land dispute resolution mechanisms.
   c Inventory of all acquired state lands and determination of outstanding compensation.

   d Policy studies on land tenure registration, divestiture of vested lands, finance and fees structure of land administration system, gender and assessment of current land administration services provided by customary land authorities.
   e Land policy development process.

2 Institutional reform and development.

   a Restructuring of public sector land agencies.
   b Decentralising and strengthening land administration services.
   c Strengthening customary land administration.
   d Strengthening private land sector institutions.
   e Strengthening land administration and management training and research institutions.

3 Improving land titling, registration, valuation and information systems.

   a Developing the cadastre and land information systems.
   b Cadastral mapping.
   c Establishing model land titling and registration offices.
   d Improving deed and title registration.
   e Land use planning and management.
   f Establishing land valuation database.
   g Piloting demarcation and registration of allodial land boundaries.
   h Piloting systematic land titling and registration.

4 Project management, monitoring and evaluation.

   a Project coordination and management.
   b Human resources development.
   c Communication strategy.
   d Monitoring and evaluation and impact assessment.

The government and development partners in the course of implementation found the original objective to be too ambitious to achieve within the five-year time frame. This resulted in project restructuring in November 2008 with modifications to the objective and outcome indicators commensurate with the time frame. The restructuring involved reallocating credit proceeds, revising the project description, adding an extra category and extending project closure from December 2008 to December 31, 2010.

The revised objective was to undertake land policy and institutional reforms and key land administration pilots for laying the foundation for a sustainable, decentralised land administration system that is fair, efficient and cost-effective and ensures land tenure security. Following the restructuring, a total of US$ 48.20 million was disbursed as against the original commitment of US$ 55.05 million, representing an 87 percent disbursement rate.

One of the major achievements of LAP 1 was the enactment of the Lands Commission Act, 2008 (Act 767), which repealed the Lands Commission Act, 1994 (Act 483) and also consequentially amended the Land Registry Act, 1962 (Act 122), Survey Act, 1962 (Act 127) and Land Title Registration Act, 1986 (PNDCL 152). Upon the coming into force of Act 767, the erstwhile Lands Commission, Land Valuation Board, Land Title Registry and Survey Department were merged into the 'new' Lands Commission with four divisions – Public and Vested Lands Management Division, Land Valuation Division, Title Registration Division, and Survey and Mapping Division. Sections 20 to 23 of Act 767 provide the functions of the four divisions of the Lands Commission. Details of other achievements of LAP 1 are presented in Table 2.1.

Act 767 exudes good intentions but some of its provisions are problematic. Thus, the provisions on Deputy Executive Secretaries. Whilst the Executive Secretary is responsible for the direction and supervision of the employees of the Commission, including the Deputy Executive Secretaries, the Act stipulates that the latter shall perform such functions as may be assigned to them by the Commission. The Commission, however, is a Constitutional creation with a Chairman at the apex and the Executive Secretary as a member with an additional responsibility for its day-to-day administration of affairs and decisions implementation (see Section 26 of Act 767).

An amendment to explicitly define the functions of the Deputy Executive Secretaries to include duties to be assigned by the Executive Secretary will cure the defect. It will not only promote good governance practices but also halt a 'difficult and mischievous' Deputy Executive Secretary seeking to misinterpret the provision for selfish gains.

The achievements implied a positive impact by LAP 1 on land administration in the country with a wide range of stakeholders including government, institutions, customary land owners and individuals as direct beneficiaries. Based on international experience, the World Bank assessed investments in policy and institutional reforms and pilot initiatives under the project as economically sound with considerable fiscal impact. For example, land-related revenues increased more than tenfold, and land sector agencies contributed more to the government's fiscal revenue than annual budget allocations to the agencies. The government demonstrated a sustained political commitment at the close of LAP 1 in December 2010, which culminated in the approval of the Project Appraisal Document (PAD) for phase 2.

Phase 2 of the project became effective on August 8, 2011, to consolidate and complete the reforms started under LAP 1 by upscaling the customary land activities and supporting the 'new' Lands Commission to streamline and computerise business processes for speedy services delivery. LAP 2 was also intended to further support the judiciary, land use planning and legal reform that began under LAP 1. The principal objective of LAP 2 was to consolidate and strengthen land administration and management systems for efficient and

Table 2.1 LAP 1 key targets and achievements

	Targets	*Baselines as of December 2003*	*Achievements*	*Remarks*
1	Turnaround time and transaction cost of registering deeds for residential plot of between 0.4 and 0.9 hectare to be reduced to not more than 1 month.	36 months	Deeds registration completed in 2.5 months (approximately 3 months).	97% improvement achieved but far less than the target; only 40% of it achieved. Turnaround time for deeds registration depended on whether land was private or public. Registration was faster for private or family land than public land that is managed by the Lands Commission because registration processes differ. The achieved turnaround time was an average of the two types of land holding. No account was made of transaction cost at the completion.
2	Turnaround time and transaction cost of registering titles for residential plot of between 0.4 and 0.9 hectare in declared title registration districts of Accra, Tema and part of Kumasi to be reduced to fewer than 6 months.	36 months	Titles registration completed between 6 and 7 months.	Cost of transaction not captured.

(*Continued*)

Table 2.1 (Continued)

	Targets	*Baselines as of December 2003*	*Achievements*	*Remarks*
3	Land litigation cases in courts in pilot areas of Wasa Amenfi, Ejisu and Gbawe to be reduced by 70%.	12 fresh disputes were recorded: Wasa Amenfi (8), Ejisu (1) and Gbawe (3).	Wasa Amenfi boundary demarcation completed and major land dispute at Anyafuri between Wasa and Denkyira resolved using an alternative dispute resolution mechanism. Boundary demarcation in Ejisu was also completed with few outstanding disputes that were referred to the Asantehene for resolution; 5 out of 8 boundary disputes were resolved. Persistent litigation between Gbawe and its adjoining allodial land owners stalled its boundary demarcation.	Conflicting judgements and a composite plan of the judgements for Gbawe and its adjoining allodial land owners were contracted out to a retired Supreme Court judge to study and provide recommendations.
4	Revenue from land transactions to both central and local government to be increased by 130%.	GH₵ 1,373,861.15 (US$ 12,229,958.23)	Total revenue of GH₵ 202,352,111.00 (US$ 134,901,407.00) mobilised, representing 147%.	Target outperformed by 17%.
5	Land titles and deeds registered by women nationwide to be increased by 50%.	288 land titles and deeds registered.	14,415 titles and 32,879 deeds registered by women. Deeds registration was also decentralised nationwide to additional 8 regions excluding Greater Accra and Ashanti Regions, which already existed.	An overwhelming achievement far in excess of the target.

6	Land Agency Act to be enacted by parliament to integrate and operationalise 6 existing land sector agencies that performed overlapping and duplicated functions into a single corporate body.	6 land sector agencies – Land Valuation Board, Lands Commission, Survey Department, Land Title Registry, Office of the Administrator of Stool Lands and Town and Country Planning Department.	Organisation, Management and Operations (OMO) studies were conducted. Lands Commission Bill enacted in December 2008 as Lands Commission Act, 2008 (Act 767). Additionally, Land Use and Spatial Planning Authority Act, 2016 (Act 925) was enacted to replace the archaic statute for the Town and Country Planning Department.	Act 767 provided a legal basis for the integration of four of the six land sector agencies into one corporate entity – the 'new' Lands Commission – comprising the Land Valuation Division, Public and Vested Lands Management Division, Survey and Mapping Division and Land Registration Division. Recommendations of the OMO studies somehow remain not implemented.
7	A consolidated Land Act was to be passed by Parliament to replace the existing laws and regulations relating to land.	166 laws and regulations.	Drafts Lands Bill developed.	The Bill was considered as a deliverable for the second phase of the project.
8	Total clearing of backlog of land related cases in the courts.	An estimation of 7,122 land litigation cases at the high courts and circuit courts nationwide.	The courts determined 6,300 cases; 88% of the target. Additionally, 9 land courts were established – 6 newly created and 3 refurbished into land courts.	Automated system implemented.
9	Policy on compensation for land compulsorily acquired by the state to be developed and preceded by an inventory of state acquired and/or occupied lands and quantum of outstanding compensation determined.	50 pilot districts selected nationwide.	Inventory[5] of state-acquired and/or -occupied land successfully completed in all 13 districts in the Central Region and additional 43 selected districts nationwide. Policy to provide guidelines for compensation or return of lands to the pre-acquisition owners also developed and approved by Cabinet.	A total of 1,144 sites were inventoried in the Central region. They included District Assembly properties – basic schools, markets, lorry parks, boreholes and cemeteries, among others. Compensation fully paid for only 160 sites. 31 selected sites in Accra revealed that only 6 had compensation fully paid.

(Continued)

Table 2.1 (Continued)

	Targets	*Baselines as of December 2003*	*Achievements*	*Remarks*
10	30 Customary Land Secretariats (CLSs) to be established for the traditional authorities; existing 2 to be refurbished and resourced. Additionally, 10 pilot land boundaries demarcation and title registration for selected allodial owners.	Only 2 for Asantehene and Gbawe traditional authority existed.	36 CLSs were established and operationalised (including Asantehene and Gbawe). Boundaries demarcation completed for 10 selected allodial owners with outstanding title registration.	Boundaries overlaps were resolved through alternative disputes resolution mechanism.
11	Cadastre and land information system to be designed and implemented as a replacement for the manual cadastre in the country. Computerised Land Information System (LIS) also to be operationalised and linked to the National Framework for Geographic Information Management.	Manual cadastre.	Phase 1 of the LIS that included an intelligent scanning of records at the Lands Commission completed. Phase 2 that included deployment of the LIS at the Lands Commission to be accomplished under LAP 2. However, a Computerised Land Use Planning and Management Information System (LUPMIS) was developed and deployed at the Land Use and Spatial Planning Authority (formerly Town and Country Planning Department). Its linkages to the LIS to be accomplished under LAP 2.	The intelligent scanning was conducted at the service providers' premises.
12	Revaluation of all properties by both public and private sector valuers in 12 pilot districts to be undertaken for rating purposes.	50,000 properties.	45,532 properties revalued; representing 91% of the target.	Private sector valuers conducted valuation and quality control by the Land Valuation Division.

Source: World Bank (2011a).

transparent land services delivery. The following key outcomes and outcome indicators were envisioned (see World Bank, 2011b):

1 Turnaround time reduced from 3 months to a maximum of 1 month for deeds registration.
2 Turnaround time reduced from 7 months to a maximum of 2 months for title registration. Information on standard statutory fees, land values and charges on land transactions were to be made readily available.
3 Application for title certificates, consents, deeds, searches, stamping and parcel plans to be made publicly available through the media, online, website and brochures.
4 Increase in the number of registered land transactions – disaggregated by gender and scale of operation, e.g., small scale vs. large scale farmers – and associated revenue.

LAP 2 therefore sought to concentrate on removing the business process bottlenecks, promoting transparency and addressing the various challenges with the aim of improving efficiency in the delivery of land services and increasing tenure security. The objective indicators were accordingly designed to particularly reduce turnaround time for titles and deeds registration, reduce costs and lead to a considerable improvement in service delivery and provision of land information to government and private sector entities.

The four components of LAP 2 were defined as:

1 *Strengthening the policy, legal and regulatory framework for land administration*: studies were to be identified to support this activity. It included work in partnership with the judiciary that aimed to reduce the level of disputes in court, partly through alternative dispute resolution (ADR) mechanisms.
2 *Improving functions and business processes for service delivery*: expectations were high for improvements to the land administration systems for statutory and customary land rights. It included policy studies to understand customary land practices and the establishment of additional Customary Land Secretariats (CLSs), and for statutory land rights, streamlining and improving the procedures for registration – largely based on the Ghana Enterprise Land Information System (GELIS) to be developed – and creating a digital backup of paper records. Backlogs for title registration to be eliminated and the time taken for issuing building permits would be reduced.
3 *Improving maps and spatial data for land administration*: included providing maps and improving the policies for mapping, surveying and the geodetic network; demarcating boundaries of customary land and private land owners; preparing land use plans; revaluation of properties; and implementing a street addressing system.
4 *Human resource development and project management*: for the disbursement of funds for project management and human resource development. It included a program to establish a communication and public awareness

strategy and its implementation. A specific sub-component was identified for mainstreaming gender equality.

LAP 2 experienced several restructurings to revise funds disbursement and also extend the closing date in April 2013 and April 2014, and again in February 2017. The restructuring concluded with a reduction in the budget from US$ 72 million to approximately US$ 50 million with subsequent major reductions in project outputs. It further ended with a major reduction in project outputs. A final restructuring in February 2018 extended the closing date to January 31, 2019, to allow for additional financing credit to be prepared and approved to complete outstanding outcome indicators, including GELIS.

In 2015, the Lands Commission established Client Service Access Units (CSAUs) in five regional capitals and two district capitals to achieve five key objectives: first, significantly reduce the turnaround time in land services delivery including plan preparation, stamp duty, official searches and issuance of land title certificates; second, reduce the cost of transacting business at the Lands Commission; third, minimise the frequency of staff and client contact; fourth, reduce staff and client frustrations; and fifth, improve transparency in land services delivery in the country. The CSAUs sought to provide an automated or digitised platform for land services delivery to replace the predominantly paper-based working environment. At the CSAUs, clients can access the Lands Commission for services via a one-stop-shop, rather than shuttling between the four divisions as had been the case in the past. The working environment is akin to a typical banking hall with a well-organised front office for clients and an onsite banking for payment of fees and charges. The CSAUs were established in Accra (Greater Accra Region), Koforidua (Eastern Region), Sekondi (Western Region), Tamale (Northern Region), Bolgatanga (Upper East Region), and Tema and Tarkwa as district offices in the Greater Accra and Western Regions, respectively.

In establishing CSAUs, the Lands Commission constituted a business process reengineering team to review and collapse flowcharts of the business processes of the four divisions of the Commission into a single workflow to be operationalised at the CSAUs. A carefully selected team of in-house staff was deployed under effective monitoring and supervision. The target was to establish a systematic, disciplined improvement platform that critically examines, rethinks and redesigns mission-delivery processes in order to achieve dramatic improvements in performance in areas important to clients and stakeholders. The process comprised three parts: first, defining new values and corporate strategies and deployment to support the new agenda; strategic steps were also taken to deal with resistance to change; second, consensus-building among clients and stakeholders such as licensed surveyors and valuers on specific changes and to agree on options available to meet their needs; and third, all aspects of the transition from current stage or business process to an improved level were planned and tested prior to implementation. All technical processes were broken down into subprocesses and activities at the four divisions of the Commission. Performance measurement of LAP 2 was largely restricted to regions with CSAUs in recognition that this intervention was the first real automation attempt for services delivery at the Lands Commission and covered the majority of high land transaction areas in the country.

The provision of an automated integrated system that would permit all divisions of the Lands Commission to share data and deliver services under the reengineered business process was envisaged under GELIS. Maps, ledgers and all other hard copies of records held by the Lands Commission were to be scanned, indexed and digitised to create an automated platform under GELIS. It was designed to work in the new reengineered business process, with the CSAUs providing a unified and digitised one-stop-shop front office for clients. GELIS was also designed to provide a platform to generate bills digitally for all services and payments at onsite banking. As project funds were depleted, the budget allocation for GELIS was drastically reduced from US$ 13 million to US$ 4 million, which limited data capturing to only four title registration districts – 01, 03, 18 and 19 – in Accra and 10 percent of data in the other four CSAU regions.

The Land Use and Spatial Planning Act, 2016 (Act 925) was enacted to establish the Land Use and Spatial Planning Authority (LUSPA) out of the Town and Country Planning Department. A new business processing manual was developed to facilitate and improve land planning applications and building permitting. The national land use framework and two regional frameworks for Greater Accra and Ashanti have since 2017 been produced by LUSPA. Key achievements under LAP 2 are presented in Table 2.2.

LAP 2 yielded quite a high financial rate of return (FRR) of 57 percent and cost-benefit ratio (CBR) of 1.97 to indicate its success that for every dollar cost incurred, a benefit of US$ 1.97 was obtained. The net present value (NPV) of US$ 492.77 million connoted a positive viable project over the 20-year period. (World Bank, 2018); an impressive overall achievement that justified LAP 2.

2.6 The path ahead

After two decades of land adminstration reforms in Ghana there are still some unresolved challenges, in particular weak land administration systems. Specifically, the turnaround time for title and deeds registration in Ghana, though competitive within sub-Saharan Africa, is globally noncompetitive per the World Bank Doing Business ranking in 2020. With an overall ranking of 118 out of 190 countries, Ghana recorded 33 days as turnaraound time for land title registration; cost of title registration at 6.1 percent of property value; five procedures for registration; and a 111th ranking in registering property. The best performer in sub-Saharan Africa was Rwanda (38 overall ranking; 3rd in registering property ranking; three procedures for property registering; and seven days turnaround time for registration and cost of title registration at 0.1 percent of property value).

Countries that made it easier to register property by reducing regulatory complexity and cost or strengthened legal institutions to account for their respective ranking in the 2020 Doing Business Report were assessed in five

Table 2.2 LAP 2 key targets and achievements on completion as of December 2018

	Targets	*Baselines as of September 2011*	*Achievements*	*Remarks*
1	Turnaround time in registering deeds in CSAU areas reduced to 1 month.	3 months.	Deeds registration completed in 2.1 months.	A marginal improvement achieved. The average turnaround time for deeds registration was 2.1 months, varying between 5.5 months in Upper East Region to 0.7 months in the Western Region. Implementation of the CSAU would have had a good impact, especially in transparency and customer satisfaction. However, there was not much investment at the back offices of the deeds registry to make sufficient changes. GELIS has not yet rolled out and it may have an impact when it is finally installed.
2	Turnaround time in registering land titles in CSAU areas reduced for subsequent transactions to 3 months.	36 months.	Indicator not available.	During preparation for the Implementation Completion and Results Report (ICR), both the baseline data and the target data were found to be unclear and inaccurately reported. The average turnaround time reported in November 2017 was 2 months, but the data was inconsistent and not accepted by the World Bank. The data was also not disaggregated according to registration of transactions and first-time registration (which takes a longer time). The Land Registration Division of the Lands Commission has huge backlogs going back many years, and these backlogs still existed. The baseline data of 7 months and the current estimates reported were not supported by facts. The only real data available came about following the introduction of the CSAUs, where document applications and processing were tracked. This had occurred since June 2016 and most of the applications had not been approved yet. The CSAUs had, however, provided greater transparency and better customer interface, but the turnaround time in title registration needed to be considered separately for first registration and subsequent transactions, and the timeframes accurately measured.

3	Basic information on standard statutory fees, land values and charges on land transactions made publicly available on 10 media platforms.	0	10 media platforms achieved.	Target achieved. Information provided in at least 10 different media, improving transparency and supporting land market activity.
4	30,000 land transactions registered.	0	82,438	Target substantially exceeded, showing greater user acceptance and participation in the land market. The indicator for measuring female participation was measured throughout the project but formally added during restructuring. Taking into account that many applications were joint (from a male/female couple) or from companies or institutions, the female participation rate was estimated at about 30 percent of the male rate. This maintained an improvement that was seen from LAP 1.
5	2 no. Legislative Instruments for Act 767 and Act 481 completed.	0	The 2 Legislative Instruments completed.	Target achieved. Legislative instruments for the Land Commissions Act and the Administrator of Stool Lands Act were finalised and passed to the Attorney General for gazetting.
6	Land Use and Spatial Planning Act prepared.	0	Act prepared.	Land Use and Spatial Planning Act, 2016 (Act 925) passed. This formed the basis for establishing the Land Use and Spatial Planning Authority (LUSPA) and the development of the national and regional strategic plans produced under the project, which in turn have guided many development projects.
7	Land Bill prepared.	0	Bill prepared.	Bill prepared, agreed by Cabinet and submitted to Parliament for consideration.
8	Customary practices ascertained in 10 areas.	8 areas	8 areas.	80 percent of target achieved and only constrained by limited funding. Customary practice documents provide very useful documentation for the training program, CLSs and development of land law and practice.

(Continued)

Table 2.2 (Continued)

	Targets	*Baselines as of September 2011*	*Achievements*	*Remarks*
9	7 Client Service Access Units (CSAUs) offices established.	0	7 CSAUs established in Accra, Koforidua, Sekondi, Tamale, Bolgatanga, Tema and Tarkwa.	CSAUs established and target fully achieved; also providing good quality customer services with greater transparency.
10	50 Customary Land Secretariats (CLSs) established.	37	51	Target outperformed. CLSs provide effective support in customary land areas to local residents, helping with information, preparing and registering documents and resolving disputes.
11	Develop an Enterprise System dubbed *The Ghana Enterprise Land Information System (GELIS)* and (i) capture data – scanning, indexing and digitising – in 5 CSAUs in Accra, Koforidua, Sekondi-Takoradi, Tamale-Savelugu and Bolgatanga; and (ii) build capacity and transfer knowledge so that local staff are able to perform data capture and system maintenance independently in the future.	0	10%	GELIS fully deployed as an integrated system that would permit all divisions of the Lands Commission to share data and contribute to joint processes. But data was captured for only four registration districts in Accra (01, 03, 18 and 19) and 10% of data in Koforidua, Sekondi-Takoradi, Tamale and Bolgatanga due to budget reduction from US$ 13 million to US$ 4 million.

12	25,000 land rights recorded at the CLSs.	1,000	36,178	Target exceeded by 44.7%.
13	79,472 backlog of land title applications cleared.	0	62,633	Good progress in clearing the backlog from 1986 to 2010, but target not fully achieved.
14	30,000 title and deeds registered.	0	82,438	Target substantially exceeded (175%), showing greater user acceptance and participation in the land market. The indicator for measuring female participation was measured throughout the project but formally added during the restructuring. Taking into account that many applications were joint (from a male/female couple) or from companies or institutions, the female participation rate was estimated at about 30 percent of the male rate. This maintained an improvement over LAP 1 achievement.
15	2,000 cases resolved by CLSs through ADR.	0	307	Target was not achieved, but there seemed little basis for setting the target in the first place. Most disagreements that would lead to a dispute appeared to be solved just by discussion at the CLS and did not get to the 'dispute' stage. Once it was a real 'dispute' it seemed that most wanted settlement by the court and ADR became unattractive.
16	2 regions for which orthophoto maps are completed.	0	2	Orthophoto maps were produced for 2 regions and used for planning, street addressing and several other uses. Topographic line maps were included within the tenders, but only 1 was produced and was rarely used.
17	5 policies for national spatial data infrastructure, survey and mapping and geodetic reference network completed.	0	5	The 5 policies were added at restructuring, completed and approved. They clearly describe the process for implementing these policies.
18	Design of the Geodetic Reference Network (GRN) Architecture for the country completed.	0	Architecture developed.	Originally planned to put the reference network in place, but funding constraints prevented it. The architecture was developed and original target to be implemented in future.

(Continued)

Table 2.2 (Continued)

	Targets	*Baselines as of September 2011*	*Achievements*	*Remarks*
19	Spatial development frameworks and regional frameworks prepared.	0	3	Target achieved. Original target was unrealistic and had to be reduced because of funding constraints. The national spatial development and two regional development frameworks developed are already guiding new major investments both nationally and regionally.
20	Boundary of 1 customary area demarcated.	0	Boundary demarcated.	Target achieved. Funding constraints necessitated the reduction in the number of boundaries demarcated from 10 to 1. Some small parts of the customary land boundaries completed remain in dispute. Many useful lessons have been learned from this exercise, which will guide future interventions.
21	2,850 streets named by sub-metro with corresponding digital database (map and text).	0	3,782	Target exceeded. The main benefit will come from improved planning, decision-making by different metro departments (including social, educational, transport, etc.) and increases in property tax collection.
22	120,000 property parcels addressed by sub-metro with corresponding digital database (map and text).	0	120,000	The digital database was developed. Accra Metropolitan Assembly (AMA) is to subsequently afix house numbers on properties.
23	Human resource development (HRD) plan completed.	Nil	HRD plan completed. Implementation of prioritised programs completed.	Fully achieved and full program implemented. This was a successful program that helped implementing agencies to fully achieve the various activities under the project.

24	100 public outreach and awareness activities undertaken.	0	111	Target exceeded. Increase in land market activities, CLS activities and participation in other project activities were helped by ensuring that public outreach activities were well-prepared and delivered.
25	4 Gender Equality Desks established for regional land sector agencies.	0	5	Target achieved. Evidence of improved gender equality demonstrated by inclusion of women in the CLS management committees and the continued improvement in the percentage of women involved in land transactions. Advisory services also provided.
26	15 civil society organisations (CSOs) trained in gender equality, land rights and monitoring and evaluation.	0	76	Target greatly exceeded. In line with other successes within training activities, there was great involvement and success in training for CSOs.
27	120 stakeholders trained (judges, lawyers, chiefs, land sector staff and CSOs)	0	5,792	Target vastly exceeded. It was particularly effective and contributed significantly to the overall success of the project.

Source: World Bank (2018).

regulatory areas. First, in the area of increased reliability of infrastructure. Croatia, Djibouti, Pakistan, Sri Lanka and Togo were the top achievers in this category. Croatia, for example, became fully digitised, increasing the efficiency and transparency of services provided by the Land Registry and Cadastre. Sri Lanka worked toward implementing a fully digital Land Registry and Survey Department by rolling out a geographical information system and also creating a single window counter for the issuance of title certificates.

Second, increased transparency of information. Globally, only 14 out of the 190 economies – Azerbaijan, Croatia, Eswatini, Gabon, Indonesia, Israel, Mauritius, Pakistan, Papua New Guinea, Rwanda, Togo, Tunisia, United Arab Emirates, and West Bank and Gaza – were distinctive. Gabon and Israel, for example, upgraded their official websites to include relevant information to the public at large regarding land registry services. Pakistan, and West Bank and Gaza began publishing online official statistics tracking the number of transactions at the immovable property registration agency.

Third, reduced property-based taxes or fees. Chad, Democratic Republic of Congo, Republic of Congo, Djibouti, Guinea and Togo were outstanding. For example, Democratic Republic of Congo reduced the cost of securing land and property titles, whilst Guinea reduced the fees to transfer property from 2 percent to 1.2 percent of the property value.

Fourth, reduced turnaround time for registering property. Ten economies (five in sub-Saharan Africa) – China, Djibouti, France, Kenya, Malawi, Malaysia, Morocco, Sri Lanka, Togo, and West Bank and Gaza – were highly rated. Malawi, for instance, made property transfer faster by decentralising the consent to transfer property to local government authorities.

Fifth, increased administrative efficiency. Eleven economies emerged as top performers – China, Djibouti, Indonesia, Israel, Kenya, Morocco, Niger, Pakistan, Senegal, Sri Lanka and Togo. Niger improved communication between the taxation department and registration department by merging procedures, making reviewing and approving property transfers significantly faster. Senegal streamlined interactions between different departments at the Property Registry.

Further interventions are required to make land administration more efficient and effective in Ghana. The following specific interventions will be relevant for future land administration reforms in the country.

Establish Continuous Operating Reference Stations to serve as the framework for base maps production

A nationwide coverage of Continuous Operating Reference Stations (CORS) as a network of Global Navigation Satellite Systems (GNSS) is required to serve as the central framework for the production of base maps. A homogenous platform for base maps production across the country should be established to also assist in other functionalities such as detection of seismic movements, change detection, disaster management and optimum route selection for emergency services such as fire, ambulance and car navigation systems.

Undertake nationwide orthophoto mapping to provide up-to-date base maps for national development

Base maps are important tools for national development, but are unfortunately inadequate in the country. These maps are needed for the development of national, regional and district spatial development frameworks, and also for land use and physical planning schemes. Additionally, they will provide inputs to establish a national cadastre that links all property ownership information to the spatial data. The maps will also serve as a monitoring tool for peri-urban development and coastal degradation.

Determine boundaries and record interests and rights of all customary owned lands

Orthophoto maps to be produced (see previous section) can be used in a ground truthing exercise to validate customary boundaries and also derive sectional maps for systematic land title registration. This will be a huge milestone to curb the current practice of sporadic title registration. This exercise will deliver an opportunity to record digitally all boundaries in addition to hardcopies.

Prepare and enforce planning schemes nationwide

Land use planning and the enforcement of planning schemes have been ineffective in Ghana. Human settlements, particularly in urban and peri-urban areas, are inefficiently guided, leading to haphazard developments and the occurrence of perennial disasters such as flooding in many cities. The processes of developing planning schemes and the issuance of building permits are cumbersome and costly. This component will address those challenges and achieve a better land use planning and control system in the country.

Deploy the Ghana Enterprise Land Information System nationwide

Though GELIS has been fully developed for the Lands Commission, it is yet to be deployed and utilised nationwide. Currently, only 10 percent of the land records have been scanned, digitised and deployed into the system due to lack of funds. It will be important to scale up without further delays to achieve the expected outcomes. The back-office activities of the Lands Commission are predominantly paper-based. Processing of clients' requests is all paper-based, and access to needed files and maps is limited. The way forward is to establish an automated platform to reduce turnaround time of services delivery for title and deeds registration, and complement the fully automated unified front office as CSAU.

Build human resource capacity and provide competitive remuneration for the land sector

Human resource capacity for land sector agencies remains inadequate and weak for want of the right mix of competent professionals. Salaries are noncompetitive and therefore, it is difficult to recruit and retain a high caliber of professionals such as Valuers, Land Administrators, Land Registrars, Lawyers and Geomatics Engineers or Land Surveyors. Currently, Valuers and Land Administrators within the Lands Commission are paid less than their colleagues in the Ghana Revenue Authority, Volta River Authority and the Social Security and National Insurance Trust. Similarly, lawyers at the Commission are paid less than their peers in the Attorney General's Department, and a similar situation prevails for Geomatic Engineers in the Commission and their colleagues in other public sector agencies. A competitive and comparable salary package for staff of the land sector agencies will promote efficiency in services delivery and serve as a motivation to eliminate rent seeking.

Build a sustainable capital base for land administration

Land administration worldwide is expensive and capital intensive. An agenda to build a solid and sustainable financial base for the Lands Commission will ultimately result in effective and efficient services delivery. Fees and charges for services should at least be cost-effective.

These interventions, when implemented, may positively impact land adminsitration in Ghana and serve as best practices for other countries with similar land administration weaknesses in sub-Saharan Africa to emulate.

Notes

1 An ethnic group in the middle and southern regions of Ghana.
2 A stool means the seat of a chief of an indigenous group or community which represents the source of authority of the chief. It is a symbol of unity, and its responsibilities devolve upon its living representatives, the chief and his councilors (elders). Land owned by such a group or community is referred to as stool land (National Land Policy, Ministry of Lands and Forestry, 1999). A skin in northern Ghana is the equivalent of a stool in southern Ghana.
3 Earth priests and land owners of communities in part of the northern regions of Ghana. This is the plural form of *tendana* (land owner).
4 The author was the Local Expert for Valuation, Land Economics and Tenure at the Ministry of Lands, Forestry and Mines for the development of the Ghana Land Administration Project Proposal in 2001, which received approval by the World Bank in 2003 for implementation as LAP 1. He was also a member of the Land Sector Technical Committee that supervised the implementation of LAP 1.
5 The author was the task team leader for the inventory exercise from 2003 to 2005.

References

Agbosu, L. (1990). Land registration in Ghana: Past, present and the future. *Journal of African Law*, 34, pp. 104–127.
Akim Abuakwa (Stool Revenue) Act, 1958 (No. 28), Ghana.

Anim-Odame, W. (2009). *Residential real estate investment in emerging economies: The case of Ghana.* Unpublished PhD Thesis, Cass Business School, Faculty of Finance, City University, London.
Deininger, K. (2003). *Land policies for growth and poverty reduction* (World Bank policy research report). Washington, DC: World Bank/Oxford University Press.
Kumasi Lands Ordinance, 1943 (Cap 145), Ghana.
Land and Native Rights Ordinance, 1927 (Cap 143), Ghana.
Land Appropriation Ordinance, 1901, Ghana.
Land Registry Act, 1962 (Act 122), Ghana.
Land Registry Ordinance, 1895, Ghana.
Land Title Registration Act, 1986 (PNDCL 152), Ghana.
Land Use and Spatial Planning Act, 2016 (Act 925), Ghana.
Lands Commission Act, 1994 (Act 483), Ghana.
Lands Commission Act, 2008 (Act 767), Ghana.
Migot-Adholla, S., Benneh, G., Place, F. and Atsu, S. (1994). Land, security of tenure, and productivity in Ghana. In: J. Bruce and S. Migot-Adholla ed., *Searching for land tenure security in Africa.* Dubuque, Iowa: Kendall/Hunt Publishing Company.
Ministry of Lands and Forestry. (1999). *National land policy.* Accra: Ministry of Lands and Forestry.
Ollennu, N. (1962). *Principles of customary land law in Ghana.* London: Sweet and Maxwell.
Public Lands Ordinance, 1876 (Cap 134), Ghana.
Republic of Ghana. (1992). *Constitution.*
Stool Lands Act, 1960 (Act 27), Ghana.
Survey Act, 1962 (Act 127), Ghana.
Toulmin, C. and Quan, J. (2000). *Evolving land rights, policy and tenure in Africa.* London: Development for International Development, DFID/IIED/NRI.
United Nations. (1948). *The universal declaration of human rights.* New York: United Nations.
Williamson, I., Enemark, S., Wallace, J. and Rajabifard, A. (2010). *Land administration for sustainable development.* Redlands, CA: ESRI Press Academic.
Woodman, G. (1988). Land title registration without prejudice: The Ghana land title registration law 1986. *Journal of African Law*, pp. 119–135.
World Bank. (2003). *Project appraisal document for Ghana land administration project.* Washington, DC: The World Bank.
World Bank. (2011a). *Implementation completion and results report on the land administration project (phase 1).* Washington, DC: The World Bank.
World Bank. (2011b). *Project appraisal document for Ghana land administration project (phase 2).* Washington, DC: The World Bank.
World Bank. (2013). *Project performance assessment report for the Ghana land administration project (phase 1).* Washington, DC: The World Bank.
World Bank. (2018). *Implementation completion and results report on the land administration project (phase 2).* Washington, DC: The World Bank.
World Bank. (2020). *Doing business report.* Washington, DC: The World Bank.

3 Legal perspectives

3.1 Introduction

This chapter covers the legal perspectives of the real estate market in the country. In particular, it deals with land acquisition, state sovereignty over land, pluralism in real estate systems, land tenure security and land-related statutes. Wherever the legal framework is inadequate and/or outdated, land administration tends to be emasculated. Many aspects of the real estate market are imbued with the law. Land and law, indeed, are inextricably linked. In Ghana, the state has access to land through its powers of eminent domain. Other land resources such as the forest reserves and mineral resources are all vested in the state. These arrangements date back to the preindependence era. The acquisition and management of lands by the state are, however, beset with challenges and sometimes result in tension between the state and pre-acquisition owners.

Governments in the past have applied powers of eminent domain to compulsorily acquire or occupy lands without any formal acquisition process. Compensation for some of these lands remains unpaid. Other related issues include non-utilisation of all the acquired land, encroachments on some acquired sites and change of use as against the purpose of acquisition. Component 1 of LAP 1 (see section 2.5) included an inventory of state-acquired and -occupied lands to inform policy formulation. A policy with guidelines on compensation or return of lands to pre-acquisition owners has since been approved by the government for implementation.

3.2 Land ownership

Land ownership is administered in a plural legal regime with statutes operating alongside customary laws and norms. Whilst it is estimated that only 20 percent of land in the country is held by government either as state or vested lands, the 80 percent residue is owned by customary authorities – stools or skins, families, clans and *tendamba*, and private individuals or entities.

State lands are acquired by the state either through compulsory acquisition or purchase and managed by the Lands Commission on behalf of the government. The state holds the absolute right in these lands and citizens may obtain up to 99 years leasehold for residential purposes and 50 years leasehold for commercial and industrial purposes. Foreigners can obtain a maximum of 50 years leasehold in all cases. This provision has always been in all Constitutions of the Republic – 1969, 1979 and 1992. Any subsequent transfer of an unexpired interest or a creation of a sublease requires a written consent of the Lands Commission.

Vested lands constitute about 2 percent of lands held by the state. When land is vested in the state, the legal title remains with the state whilst the equitable or beneficiary interest resides in the stool. Reasons for the vesting include land use planning, as in the case of North Dzorwulu in Accra; chieftaincy and land litigations, for example, as in Sunyani, Nkawkaw and Winneba; and political, as in the classic case of Kumasi Town lands (part 1 lands). Institutional and legal structures have been put in place for the management of vested lands. The Lands Commission is mandated to manage these lands on behalf of the state. Revenues accruing from vested lands are, however, disbursed to beneficiary stools in line with the formula stipulated by Article 267 of the Constitution. Devesting of stool lands, particularly those vested in government on political points, will reduce the level of distrust and tensions between customary authorities and government.

Stool lands under Article 295 (1) of the Constitution include any land, or interest in or right over any land, controlled by a stool or skin, the head of a particular community or the captain of a company for the benefit of the subjects of that stool or the members of that community or company. Stool and skin lands are therefore community lands vested in the various customary authorities or elders in trust for the community. The fiduciary principle underlying this definition is reinforced in Article 36 (8), which provides that the state shall recognise that ownership and possession of land carry a social obligation to serve the larger community and, in particular, the state shall recognise that the managers of public, stool, skin and family lands are fiduciaries charged with the obligation to discharge their functions for the benefit respectively of the people of Ghana and of the stool, skin or family concerned, and are accountable as fiduciaries in this regard.

Furthermore, Article 267 (3) stipulates that there shall be no disposition or development of any stool land unless the Regional Lands Commission of the region in which the land is situated has certified that the disposition or development is consistent with the development plan drawn up or approved by the planning authority for the area concerned. In effect, the key to any disposition or development of any stool or skin land is an approved development plan by the planning authority for the area concerned. Such alienation must therefore be supported by the concurrence of the Lands Commission to make it valid. The stool or skin occupant manages such lands and holds the absolute rights. These lands are vested in the appropriate stool on behalf of, and in trust for, the subjects of the stool in accordance with customary law and usage.

Family or clan lands are those owned by families or clans in the community. These are considered private properties because the owners possess the freehold interests from which they create leaser interests. This category is very limited in stock but prominent in some regions including Volta, Eastern, Greater Accra, Oti, Western and Central.

All customary sources of land tenure and rights as well as those derived from common law are duly recognised as legitimate sources of title to land. Tenure and rights recognised by common law include allodial, customary freehold, leasehold, share cropping and other customary tenancies. There is however, a high incidence of insecurity of land tenure due to challenges such as conflicts of interests between and within customary land-owning groups and the state, land racketeering, delays by courts in adjudicating land cases and weak land administration systems (see earlier discussion). Policy guidelines needed to address the challenges have been enunciated in the National Land Policy; see Box 3.1.

Land consists of a 'bundle' of rights that defines the nature of legitimate uses and benefits to be derived. Land acquisition provides the owner with several rights and interests over the land; for example, the right to occupy, the right to build on it, the right to mortgage and the right to sublet or assign. Combinations of these rights are possible and may be associated with the duration of the rights. The duration for the use and enjoyment of the interests and rights in the land is important.

In Ghana, allodial is the highest title capable of being held in land, subject only to such restrictions or limitations or obligations imposed by general laws of the state. It is the absolute ownership of land where the holder owes no obligation to a superior. Thus, it confers on its holder a complete and absolute freedom to deal with the land. In the past, the acquisition of allodial title was by conquest and subsequent settlement thereon, or by discovery by hunters or pioneers of the stool or skin or by a gift or purchase. Currently, the only way an allodial title may be acquired is either by purchase or gift, since the acquisition by conquest is now an impossibility. Specifically, there are three ways in which an allodial title may be transferred:

(i) Compulsory acquisition under the State Lands Act, 1962 (Act 125).
(ii) Through a gift.
(iii) Purchase by another stool (skin), family, community or individual.

An interest of uncertain duration is termed a freehold. It is an interest that is carved out of an allodial holding and subsequently held for an indefinite period. A freehold interest is accordingly lesser than allodial in theory. Freeholders can transfer such interest to their heirs. So long as there is someone who claims succession in title from the original freeholder, the freehold title will continue. Nonetheless, in the event of a freehold title coming to an end without a successor, the title shall be merged with the allodial title from which it was originally carved. In the past, there was a hybrid of freehold interest known as a customary freehold. This is an interest in land that was acquired by a person by reason of being a subject of a stool, skin or member of a family.

Box 3.1 Abridged Policy guidelines on security of land tenure and rights in the National Land Policy, 1999

a Decision-making with respect to disposal of land should take into consideration the natural resources of the land, conservation of land for the future generation, protection of land rights of the present generation and accountability to the subjects for whom the land is held in trust, in accordance with the provisions of the Administration of Lands Act, 1962 (Act 123) and the Head of Family Accountability Act, 1985 (PNDCL 112).

b No interest in or right over any land belonging to an individual, family, clan, stool or skin can be compulsorily acquired without payment of fair, adequate and prompt compensation.

c The best evidence of title to land, in any area declared as a land title registration district, is the Land Title Certificate issued in accordance with the provisions of the Land Title Registration Act, 1986 (PNDCL 152). In areas not declared land title registration districts, instruments registered under the Land Registry Act, 1962 (Act 122) should be sufficient proof of title.

d As much as possible, land disposal or acquisition of any kind for all types of land uses should not render a land title holder, his kith and kin, and descendants completely landless or tenants on the land to which they originally had legitimate title, save in the case of compulsory acquisition in the public interest.

e Tenants of land anywhere in Ghana are obliged to respect the customary or common law covenants governing the tenancy of land of which they are tenants.

f. Where land has been allocated to a government or public organisation, neither that organisation nor the Lands Commission can alienate that land or part of it to a third party in the public interest without consultation with the Sector Minister; and

g Buildings, structures or substructures on lands to which the developer or owner has no title or development/building permit may be demolished at the cost of the developer.

Such a person has a customary right to freely use part of stool's, skin's or family's land that was not occupied by another person and therefore not an interest which lies in a grant. In contrast, a stranger to a stool, skin or family in Ghana cannot, under any circumstances, occupy stool, skin or family land as of right.

Since 1992, Article 267 (5) has, in effect, abolished freehold interests carved out of stool lands. The only interest which can be created out of stool land after 1992 is a leasehold or some lesser interests. Since Article 267 (5) is not expressed to have retrospective effect, freehold interests created before the coming into effect of the Constitution are not affected. Currently, any attempt to create a freehold interest out of stool land cannot be valid on account of Article 267 (5) and shall confer no interest whatsoever on the transferee.

A lease is an interest in land created to last for a fixed period. It is created when the owner, known as the lessor, conveys a possessory interest in the land to another, the lessee, for a specific duration in exchange for a valuable consideration. Every lease requires a date on which it commences and a date on which it must expire. There can be no lease if the date of commencement and date of expiration cannot be precisely ascertained. It creates a contract and special relationship of landlord and tenant between the lessor and lessee. When the leasehold is of a short duration, for instance, weekly, monthly or yearly, it is commonly known as a tenancy, contrary to a lease of longer duration. The parties enjoy the privilege of arms-length negotiations in concluding the transaction. The legal principle of *caveat emptor*, however, holds, where the onus lies on purchasers to be fully aware of what they were paying for.

Where a formal deed of lease had been executed showing the terms of the contract, no antecedent or subsequent negotiations are admissible to construe the contract. Another incidence of a lease is the fact that a contract is void *ab initio* if it is expressly or impliedly prohibited by statute or other law. Also, a lease is void *ab initio* if it is contrary to public policy. Absolutely, there should be no intent to perform an illegality at the time of executing a lease. The parties are expected to carefully decide on what they want in the deed of lease and be able to strike a balance between language specificity and flexibility. Generally, it is not a good practice to leave too many terms open for further interpretations. The basic essentials necessary to characterise a transaction as a lease must include:

Parties and capacity: There must be a willing lessor and a willing lessee as the parties. The parties must be mentally competent, of legal age and clothed with the capacity to execute the lease. In Ghana, 18 years or above constitutes the legal age. Parties must be sane, and the legality of the purpose of the lease must also be met. Both parties must sign the document with witnesses to satisfy the principle of offer and acceptance. Properties purchased in favour of a minor must be treated and held by a trustee or trustees in trust for the beneficiary. Never should a minor be made to execute a lease transaction. If two or more persons are either the lessors or lessees, all must sign the document.

Description of the land: The land must be clearly described in the schedule of the lease to avoid future dispute. The description must include the dimensions of the land and its size in acreage appropriately stated together with a parcel or cadastral plan depicting the land as a polygon.

Consideration: The law requires an exchange of consideration where the owner gives up title to the land in return for money, and the purchaser gives up money – valuable consideration – in return for title to the land. Remember, the practice in Ghana is that the purchaser normally pays a lump sum as a premium or customarily referred to as '*drink money*' and in addition is required to pay annual ground rent, which has to be nominal and usually paid in advance. Both the premium and ground rent must be agreed upon and clearly stated in the lease. The lessee is expected to be certain about what is being paid for, especially in dealing with chiefs and private parties. Also, parties are encouraged to pay attention to the statutory requirements when payment for an interest in land is being made. Unless stipulated to the contrary, the rent is due on the date set for payment. The practice is a monthly, quarterly or annual payment of ground rent. Bargaining is an acceptable behaviour; parties must therefore bargain strongly and honestly.

Duration of lease: A lease is a terminable interest, with a definite term expressed as number of years, for which the interest and rights in the land can be enjoyed or exercised. The commencement and expiration dates must both be stated. Typically, the term is between 50 and 99 years certain for Ghanaians for residential purposes, and up to 50 years for commercial purposes. It is recommended that a renewal clause for the lease term is agreed upon and explicitly stated. Article 266 (4) provides that no interest in, or right over, any land in Ghana shall be created which vests in a person who is not a citizen of Ghana a leasehold for a term of more than 50 years at any one time. This provision is therefore of great importance in negotiating lease terms, particularly for non-Ghanaians.

At common law, a lease for a fixed term comes to an end when that term expires without the need for notice from either party. However, a lease may contain a clause that allows the lessee to renew the lease every time it expires. It is expected that the lease would be renewed on same terms and conditions as contained in the expired lease with the exception of a new rent to be mutually agreed upon by the parties. Usually, the renewal clause is provided as an option to be exercised by the lessee. The lessee is therefore required to take the following six steps:

1 Know when the lease expires.
2 Carefully read the lease; highlight the renewal clause and exercise the option to renew by applying to the Executive Secretary or respective Regional Lands Officer of the Lands Commission (for state and vested lands) or the lawful representative of the stool, skin, clan, family, tendana or individual.
3 Negotiate with the lessor for the renewal.
4 Decide and communicate your decision to the lessor.

5 Carefully study the new lease to ensure that all agreed upon terms and conditions have been captured.
6. Execute the new lease and register at the Lands Commission (see registration processes in section 3.5).

3.3 Securing your interest in land

The principle of *caveat emptor*, which literally means 'let the buyer beware,' is relevant in ensuring secure interest in land. It requires due diligence for which the prospective lessee or purchaser must know that:

- The burden is on the lessee (purchaser) to confirm that the location, condition and nature of the land are all suitable for the intended purpose.
- It is the responsibility of the lessee (purchaser) to ensure that there are no conflicting claims or defects in the title.

Due diligence is therefore important. A physical inspection of the land should be undertaken. The prospective lessee must conduct an official search at the Lands Commission, using a copy of the parcel or cadastral plan particularly, at the Land Registration Division, and Public and Vested Lands Management Division. A title search will reveal root of title or ownership history, the chain of title to the land. An examination of the search report will show whether the lessor (vendor) has good title to transfer or not.

All related documents, including court judgements (where applicable), must be studied to form an opinion, and as much as possible, seek professional advice from a Land Economist, Valuer or lawyer. Ensure that all undertakings, promises and assurances by the government, customary authorities or private parties are in writing and enforceable. Lease terms and conditions should be explained to parties – vendor and vendee – as well as witnesses. Insist that chiefs or family heads execute transactions in the presence of at least two principal elders.

Besides the Lands Commission, a search using the parcel or cadastral plan must be conducted at the respective Metropolitan, Municipal and District Assembly (MMDA) to ascertain the permissible use for the plot. When you purchased an already registered land, you can be sure of minimising the associated risks. The *nemo dat quod non habet* principle, which literally means 'you cannot give what you do not have,' is another cardinal principle that must always be adhered to. Simply, the purchase of a land from someone who has no ownership right to it denies the purchaser any ownership title. It further means one cannot transfer to another more rights and interests than they possess. The *nemo dat rule* also requires due diligence. It is always safe and prudent to deal with the true owners only. The potential lessee must ensure that the purported interest holder is clothed with the capacity to transfer title. The interest holder should also possess all relevant documents covering the land and make them available for inspection. The name(s) in the documents must be consistent with the owner(s)' identity. Once again, seek professional advice from a Land Economist, Valuer or lawyer. If the land is described as state land, then all enquiries must be made at the Lands Commission. Check if the land has been properly acquired and compensation fully paid. This is one major source of tension and conflict between some lessees of government and customary authorities.

3.4 Defective land title and actions needed

Land title deficiency is not uncommon and can be tricky. It is problematic because a large number of people have concluded transactions purported to be leaseholds with hard- earned income only to realise their title to the land was defective. There is, however, hope, with a 50–50 chance to regularise title subject to the availability of the land. But merely occupying the land does not provide sufficient evidence for title regularisation. Five decisive steps are to be taken in the case of stool, skin or family lands.

First, conduct two searches at the Lands Commission: at the Public and Vested Lands Management Division, and Land Registration Division. Both searches can be conducted concurrently. As stated earlier, these search reports will reveal historical records information on the land. Certainly, you will require professional advice on the search reports to highlight your chances.

Second, identify and negotiate with the legitimate stool occupant or family head. Payment of a premium (*drink money*) should be anticipated, but the quantum of amount will definitely depend on your negotiation skills and/or referrals (if any). Insist that two principal elders sit in all negotiations through to payment and execution of a fresh lease in your favour.

Third, a valid deed of lease must be executed and the lease should not have erasures or blank spaces to be filled in later in ink. Ensure that copies of the parcel or cadastral plans in the document are barcoded – signed by a licensed surveyor, approved by the Director of Survey and Mapping Division and affixed with a barcode on the rear side.

Fourth, request for right of entry if you are not in occupation. This step is essential because the deed of lease will necessarily have a covenant that seeks to provide the lessee with quiet and peaceable enjoyment of the land.

Fifth, proceed to the Lands Commission to register the land for a secure title (this process is discussed further under section 3.5).

From previous discussion we know that 20 percent of the stock of land in the country is state and vested lands. For this category, an absence of a good title simply means one has encroached on a state or vested land, which requires an application to the Lands Commission for regularisation. This responsibility may or may not yield a successful outcome. Regularisation is possible if the Executive Instrument for the acquisition has been revoked or amended as in the case of the Abeka Lapaz Sports Complex land in Accra. The second possibility is where there is an encroachment on a plot within an area already zoned for the same land use; for instance, an encroachment (residential building) on a land originally zoned for residential purposes or an encroachment (commercial building) on land zoned for commercial purposes. Again, it is dependent on the plot being unencumbered and free to be allocated.

An application for regularisation of title in respect to such lands must be made with a copy of the defective lease to the Lands Commission for consideration. Photographs showing occupation should be attached and the duration of occupation stated. The encroacher's situation raises the possibility that two requirements are fulfilled – holding a defective title and applicant in occupation of the land for a reasonable period of time, five years or more. On receiving an application for regularisation, the Lands Commission will review the claim and physically inspect the property for validation, which will culminate in its decision. Notification of the decision – approval or rejection – will be communicated to the applicant. Approval in the form of an offer letter will include penalty, premium, annual rent and other charges to be paid in full by a stipulated time. The applicant is expected to make payments of the premium, ground rent and penalty and accept the offer with copies of receipts attached. The Lands Commission, on receipt of the acceptance letter, will invite the applicant to complete an appropriate form and questionnaire with passport photo to pave the way for lease preparation, execution and readiness for registration. A rejection means the lease cannot be regularised and the encroacher must take steps to vacate the land.

3.5 Processes of land registration

A registered land document provides evidence in support of a claim to a property. Registration may therefore be described as the best way to protect your land. In Ghana, two systems of land registration apply: title registration in the Greater Accra Region and part of the Ashanti Region including neighbourhoods such as Adum, Ahodwo, Anwomaso, Asokwa, Asuoyeboa, Ayeduse Ayigya, Boadi, Bohyen, Breman, Dakodwom, Fumesua, Kaase, Kotei, Kwadaso, Manhyia, Patasi, Santasi, Suame, Tafo, and Tanoso; and deeds registration in all other parts of the country.

Processes for title registration

- Read the document and be satisfied with the terms and conditions.
- Ensure the document is duly signed, witnessed and oath of proof sworn at the high court with no erasures or gaps to be filled in ink.
- Ensure that the parcel or cadastral plan in the document is duly signed by a licensed surveyor, approved by Director of Survey and Mapping Division or Regional Surveyor and barcoded.
- Ensure you satisfy requirements in the checklist of the Lands Commission (checklist provided in the Appendix).

- Submit document (usually three copies) for stamp duty assessment and pay at the Client Services Access Unit (CSAU) at the Lands Commission, Cantonments in Accra, district office of the Land Registration Division in Tema or Lands Commission Office near the Golden Tulip Hotel in Kumasi.
- Submit the original copy of the document for registration and pay statutory fees that are generated digitally at the Client Services Access Unit (CSAU) in Accra, district office in Tema or Lands Commission Office in Kumasi.
- Keep date of acknowledgement slip in your diary for follow ups.
- Title certificate will be issued on completion and applicant invited to sign for collection at the CSAU or point of submission in Tema or Kumasi.

Upon the issuance of land title certificate, the state guarantees that the information on the land in the register held at the Lands Commission is correct. This is in line with the insurance principle of title registration, which states that 'the state is responsible for the veracity of the register and for providing compensation in the case of errors or omissions, thus providing financial security for the owners.'

Processes for deeds registration

- Read the document and be satisfied with the terms and conditions.
- Ensure the document is duly signed, witnessed and oath of proof sworn at the high court with no erasures or gaps to be filled in ink.
- Ensure that the parcel or cadastral plan in the document is duly signed by a licensed surveyor and approved by the Director of Survey and Mapping or Regional Surveyor.
- Ensure you satisfy requirements in the checklist of the Lands Commission.
- Submit document (usually three copies) for stamp duty assessment and pay at the Regional Office of the Land Valuation Division of the Lands Commission.
- Submit document (usually three copies) for registration and pay statutory fees at Regional Office of the Public and Vested Lands Management Division of the Lands Commission.
- Keep date of acknowledgement slip in your diary for follow ups.
- Obtain a tax clearance certificate when the deed is ready for the issuance of a registration number.
- Original copy of deed with a registration number will be released to the applicant on completion.

All efforts must be made to accelerate title registration nationwide. There is a cost to buying land; but there is a greater cost for not registering it. When lessees fail to duly register their lands, they are deemed to have denied themselves of ownership rights.

3.6 Regulatory framework

A regulatory framework that provides a clear and consistent set of land administration policies and laws is needed for the real estate market. There is an existing plethora of conflicting and obsolete land laws and regulations in the statute books. Some judicial decisions on land- related cases are also conflicting. The existence of some 166 state laws that regulate land administration and establish public land sector institutions is sometimes used to confuse issues, delay implementation of activities and prolong the determination of land cases in court.

To address these issues, a revision of the national land policy and codification of the numerous land-related laws will be required. An Act of Parliament on land with the primary objective to revise and consolidate the laws on land, harmonise those laws to ensure sustainable land administration and management, provide effective land tenure and provide for related matters should be promoted and wholly supported to specifically address the deficiencies. Benefits to be achieved will include:

1 *Improved tenure security*: this will reduce risks such as land grabbing, encroachment, land disputes and expropriation. Lack of tenure security has been identified as a contributory factor to poverty among the citizenry and also as a restraining force to national development.
2 *Increased land-related investment from both domestic and foreign sources*: investors' confidence will be boosted as a result of a secure, stable and predictable investment environment. This will also improve access to credit.
3 *Improved efficiency of land resource use*: this benefit will stimulate the formal development of rural markets and the growth of urban land markets with a consequential effect on national development.
4 *Improved information on land transactions*: land valuation system that thrives on credible data will be developed to promote land-related tax collection at the Lands Commission and Ghana Revenue Authority. Land use planning system at MMDAs will also be improved with an integrated database.

A fully functioning regulatory framework can stimulate the real estate market in Ghana to enhance socioeconomic activities. The legal and institutional regulations, international standards, ethical rules and best practices must therefore be consistent to anchor the economy.

References

Administration of Lands Act, 1962 (Act123), Ghana.

Anim-Odame, W. (2009). *Residential real estate investment in emerging economies: The case of Ghana*. Unpublished PhD Thesis, Cass Business School, Faculty of Finance, City University, London.

Atwood, D. A. (1990). Land registration in Africa: The impact on agricultural production. *World Development*, 18 (5), pp. 659–671.

AUC-ECA-AfDB Consortium. (2011). *Land policy in Africa, West Africa regional assessment.* Addis Ababa: United Nations Economic Commission for Africa.

Card, R., Murdoch, J. and Murdoch, S. (1994). *Law for estate management students.* 4th ed. London: Butterworths.

Da Rocha, B. and Lodoh, C. (1995). *Ghana land law and conveyancing.* Accra: Anansesem Publications.

Dale, P. and McLaughlin, J. (2003). *Land administration.* Oxford: Oxford University Press.

Head of Family Accountability Act, 1985 (Act112), Ghana.

Karp, J. and Klayman, E. (2006). *Real estate law.* 6th ed. Chicago: Dearborn Real Estate Education.

Land Registry Act, 1962 (Act 122), Ghana.

Land Title Registration Act, 1986 (PNDCL 152), Ghana.

Ministry of Lands and Forestry. (1999). *National land policy.* Accra: Ministry of Lands and Forestry.

Republic of Ghana. (1969). *Constitution.*

Republic of Ghana. (1979). *Constitution.*

Republic of Ghana. (1992). *Constitution.*

Stamp Duty (Amendment) Act, 2008 (Act 764), Ghana.

Toulmin, C. and Quan, J. (2000). *Evolving land rights, policy and tenure in Africa.* London: DFID/IIED/NRI.

William, I. (1997). *Essential land law.* 2nd ed. London: Cavendish Publishing Limited.

Woodman, G. (1988). Land title registration without prejudice: The Ghana land title registration law 1986. *Journal of African Law*, pp. 119–135.

World Bank. (2003). *Project appraisal document for Ghana land administration project.* Washington, DC: The World Bank.

4 Market dynamics

4.1 Introduction

Surging global real estate capital flows have been a major factor in the development of a set of 'emerging' real estate markets in Asia, Latin America and Central and Eastern European countries. For countries in sub-Saharan Africa, the impact has been less significant. By international standards, real estate markets in sub-Saharan Africa have remained small with the exception of South Africa. Markets which are small in total value are less likely to offer investments in large lot sizes, or the levels of liquidity preferred by international investors. A standard measure of real estate market transparency in the industry is the Global Real Estate Transparency Index (GRETI) by Jones Lang LaSalle (JLL). The index covers factors such as performance measurement, market fundamentals, governance of listed vehicles, regulatory and legal, transaction process including availability of market information, and sustainability.

Market transparency is the foundation that allows investors and corporate occupiers to operate and make decisions with confidence in the real estate market. It supports governments and institutions to function effectively, providing long-term benefits to stakeholders and the public at large. Without transparency, real estate markets are unattractive and inefficient.

A regional trend analysis of GRETI shows that transparency broadens across USA simply because of regulatory improvements and enhanced data collection that underpin the progress. Asia Pacific continues to show the strongest improvement, supported by record levels of real estate investments. Real estate markets in Central and Eastern European countries continue to advance as they catch up with their Western peers. The Middle East and North Africa, with Dubai typically setting the pace in the subregion, present a host of government initiatives and increasing dynamics in the real estate technology industry. In sub-Saharan Africa, limited progress in terms of data availability and improved transaction processes have been recorded.

The real estate market in Ghana ranked 76th by GRETI and together with Nigeria (67th), Ecuador (79th), Rwanda (78th), Uruguay (72nd) and Pakistan (75th) were in 2018 classified as low transparent. South Africa is a transparent real estate market and is ranked 21st globally. Markets in sub-Saharan

Africa continue to demonstrate limited progress but with improvements in Nigeria and Kenya where market data availability has improved. Valuation standards in these two countries have also been made consistent with international practices. Ghana and Nigeria have accelerated online publication of market data to promote the real estate market.

The real estate markets in Accra and Tema form the largest conurbation in the country. Accra is the largest city in Ghana and also is the national capital, with an estimated population of 2.3 million (Ghana Statistical Service, 2010). Accra is well placed as a potential business and financial hub in sub-Saharan Africa. Economic activities in the country are increasingly concentrated in Accra and evident by land values that are half or a little above in other urban centres. Peripheral areas along the eastern, western and northern corridors outside Accra continue to experience huge pressure of conversion of agricultural lands into new residential neighbourhoods. Tema, with a population of 353,086 is the county's largest port and major industrial centre. Tema lies to the southeast of Accra and is only 18 kilometres away; together, the two cities form the dominant commercial and industrial conglomeration in Ghana.

Kumasi, the second-largest city, is 248 kilometres north of Accra with a population[1] of 2 million. It is the capital of the Ashanti Region and known as the garden city. The city is characterised by rapid urbanisation and scarcity of residential properties. Capital and rental values are generally high relative to other urban cities except Accra. Sekondi-Takoradi is a twin city of 539,548 population as of 2010. It is 226 kilometres from Accra and is the capital of the Western Region. The oil discovery in the region continues to attract more people, with rapid population growth that has resulted in an increased demand for residential and office accommodation. Koforidua is the capital of the Eastern Region with a population of 122,300. Its real estate market is predominantly residential, with offices generally limited to government Ministries, Departments and Agencies (MDAs).

The real estate market in the country has continued to receive very little attention from researchers and policy-makers, and unsurprisingly has been dominated by domestic investors but with huge potentials for foreign investors. Other mitigating factors include a high urbanisation rate, a lack of access to transaction data, a high cost of building materials and a limited mortgage market. This nascent real estate market is disaggregated into residential, office, retail and industrial submarkets.

4.2 Residential market

The residential market is characterised by excess demand over supply, yielding a cumulative deficit estimated at 1.7 million (see Owusu-Ansah *et al.*, 2019). There is a national housing policy, which aims at 'creating viable and sustainable communities through the provision of adequate, decent and affordable housing that is accessible and sustainable to satisfy the needs of Ghanaians.' The fundamental role of government is to provide an enabling environment by extending key infrastructure and encouraging private sector developers to champion housing delivery (Ministry of Water Resources, Works and Housing, 2015).

The market can be conveniently classified into formal and informal, with the former seen as well-structured and with conformity of developments to planning schemes. Access roads within neighbourhoods are provided together with utility services as basic infrastructure. The informal market, in contrast, generally has low-quality properties, high occupancy, inadequate utility services and poor access roads.

The private sector has continued to deliver a large proportion of the country's rented residential stock. In the Greater Accra Region, 29 percent of households live in private, rented residential accommodations. A further small group (13 percent) lives in owner-occupied buildings, with a large portion (58 percent) of shared premises with relatives on a rent-free basis (Ghana Statistical Service, 2010). There is a sizeable state rent-free sector providing accommodation for civil and public servants, which accounts for 19.9 percent of households in Accra. A fairly large percentage (38.2 percent) of households in Accra is classified as owner-occupiers. In other urban centres such as Kumasi, Takoradi, Koforidua, Cape Coast and Sunyani, a greater proportion of households (42.3 percent) own their residential accommodations, 34.5 percent live in rented premises and 23.2 percent enjoy rent-free houses. Nationwide, 57.4 percent and 22.1 percent of the households are owner-occupiers and renters, respectively. The remaining 20.5 percent are rent-free occupiers.

Much of the residential development in the formal markets of Accra and Tema has been promoted by government policies such as the establishment of the Ghana Real Estate Developers Association (GREDA), which aims to provide an enabling environment for public and private sector cooperation. GREDA draws together representatives of government departments, real estate professional bodies, brokers and major developers to coordinate public policy and private developers to promote the supply of new residential units. Members of GREDA have been the major corporate suppliers of new residential investments and also contributed extensively towards the residential markets' development in Accra, Tema, Kumasi and other regional capitals. State agencies such as TDC Company Limited (formerly Tema Development Corporation), State Housing Company (SHC) and the Social Security and National Insurance Trust (SSNIT) are also prominent developers of residential stock for sale and rental in the formal sector. These are state owned institutions with a sizeable portfolio of residential units.

Typically, residential leases are drafted with covenants that put the responsibility on tenants for routine maintenance and payments of utility costs. This leaves landlords' outgoings limited to costs relating to management and major structural and external works, estimated at 7 percent of annual rental income; property rates, which vary with location and pegged up to 1.4 percent of annual rent; and ground rents averaged at 0.3 percent of annual rent. Total deductions from gross rents are therefore estimated at 8.7 percent minimum of annual rent excluding residential rental income tax at 8 percent of gross income. No information is available on the prevalence or costs of property insurance, which would fall upon landlords. But anecdotal evidence suggests that it is not a common practice for landlords to insure residential properties.

Five residential investment submarkets can be classified in Accra in line with the residential zoning typology of the Ministry of Local Government (see Ministry of Local Government, 1990), allotting to each zone titles which reflect the overall status. Box 4.1 presents a summary of the typology based on a large set of neighbourhood characteristics including type of residential stock, plot sizes, quality of infrastructure and availability of amenities. Residential investment submarkets are defined as Upmarket, Gated market, Emerging upmarket, Working-class market and Low-end market. The classification is deemed appropriate and a better substitute for income-based residential classification such as 'high-, middle- and low-income' residential submarkets.

The neighbourhoods for Upmarket in Accra include Airport Residential, Cantonments, East Legon, Labone, Ridge and Roman Ridge. These were originally developed exclusively for owner-occupation by senior public officers, expatriates and other Ghanaian elites. Residential units in these neighbourhoods in the past occupied large plots with long, secure leaseholds from

Box 4.1 Residential submarkets in Accra

1 **Upmarket:** This includes Airport Residential, Cantonments, East Legon, Labone, Ridge, Ringway Estate, Roman Ridge and Switchback Road.

Neighbourhood characteristics:
State owns freehold interest in land; low-density buildings predominantly of detached types; plot sizes of not less than 600 square metres; spacious environment free from intrusion by incompatible land uses; community facilities such as schools, clinics and corner shops adequately provided; roads and concrete drains; and public utility services adequately provided.

2 **Gated market:** Including East Airport (Golden Gate), East Legon Extension (Trasacco Villas), Gemini Court, Imperial Homes and Taysec Garden.

Neighbourhood characteristics:
Customary freeholders in land; gated community with high-density buildings; spacious environment free from intrusion by incompatible land uses; access roads and concrete drains available; and public utility services adequately provided.

3 **Emerging upmarket:** This includes Abelemkpe, Dzorwulo, East Legon Extension, North Legon and West Legon.

Neighbourhood characteristics:
Both state and customary freeholds in land; predominantly detached with varied plot sizes; spacious environment; no intrusion by incompatible land uses; community facilities such as schools, clinics and corner shops adequately provided; and surfaced roads and concrete drains with basic public utility services.

4 **Working-class:** Achimota, Adenta, Baatsona, Dansoman, Dome, Okpoigono, Kaneshie and Teshie/Nungua Estates.

Neighbourhood characteristics:
State and customary freeholders; variety of buildings at net site densities of between 15 and 45 units per hectare; a mixture of house types (detached, semidetached, etc.); small-scale retail development in selected areas; and adequate level of infrastructural and social amenities.

5 **Low-end market:** Newtown, Madina, Kotobabi, Korle Gonno, Teshie, Labadi, Nungua and Bubuashie.

Neighbourhood characteristics:
State and customary freeholders; wide range of buildings with various constructional details and of low quality, characterised by traditional buildings dated by several decades; and inadequate infrastructural and social amenities.

the state. With an influx of international and local businesses, these areas have in recent years evolved into mixed-used neighbourhoods. The most recent residential construction has taken the form of subdivisions, where 'colonial' bungalows on large plots are redeveloped into higher density, semidetached townhouses and apartments. Urban renewal interventions have been employed to transform property characteristics and skylines of cities including Accra, Kumasi, Takoradi and Tema.

Increasingly, developers are looking for 'brownfield' sites to execute redevelopment schemes and transform the neighbourhoods. Land prices have accordingly increased noticeably over the last decade and averaged at US$ 3 million per acre in the Upmarket including Airport Residential, Cantonments, Labone, Ridge and Roman Ridge in Accra. Newer residential neighbourhoods with limited building land such as Airport Hills, East Airport, East Legon Hills, West Legon, East Legon Extension (Adjirigano) and Burma Hills are increasingly becoming popular as Emerging upmarket.

Townhouses and penthouses in the Upmarket are the most expensive properties of between US$ 300,000 and US$ 2 million price bracket. Generally, prices and rents are quoted in US dollars but payable in Cedis (local currency). Apartments average between US$ 100,000 and US$ 400,000 depending on the number of bedrooms. Rental values are in the range of US$ 3,500 to US$ 8,000 per month, payable in advance for townhouses and penthouses. For apartments, monthly rents payable in advance are between US$ 1,500 and US$ 4,000. Gross yield on residential investment in the Upmarket is between 9 percent and 14 percent. Land values are expected to stabilise as a high supply of apartments and their relatively high prices have resulted in a limited number of sales or letting transactions.

Emerging upmarket and Gated communities are characterised by single-family homes and apartments of one- to four-bedroom units in the range of US$ 200,000 to US$ 800,000, depending on the quality of the vicinity. Prices of similar properties in the Working-class neighbourhoods in Accra and other urban cities are discounted approximately between 20 percent and 40 percent. Overconcentration of developers in the Upmarket, Gated communities and Emerging upmarket accounts for the excess supply.

The Working-class neighbourhoods in Accra include Kaneshie, Dansoman, Teshie-Nungua Estate, Achimota, Dome, Ashongman, Adenta, Haatso and Tantra Hill. The market is characterised by detached and semidetached (expandable or non-expandable) units, typically priced between US$ 35,000 and US$ 300,000. Rental values range between US$ 150 per month and US$ 2,000 per month. Gross yields for this submarket range from 6 percent to 10 percent depending on the investment characteristics. Owner-occupied residential properties are prevalent. The Low-end market is distinguished by a mixture of old, traditional and refurbished buildings of low-quality constructional details, largely of owner-occupation and high density. Neighbourhoods in this category include Bubuashie, Labadi, Jamestown, Odorkor, Abofu, Teshie, Nungua, Kwashieman and Accra Newtown.

Residential market in Kumasi may be categorised into Upmarket, Working-class and Low-end. Neighbourhoods such as Danyame, Parakou Estates within Atasamanso, West Nhyiaeso, Nhyiaeso and Ridge constitute the Upmarket. Prices of residential properties range between US$ 100,000 and US$ 400,000, depending on the number of bedrooms and location. Rental values per month for a two- to four-bedroom property range between US$ 1,000 and US$ 2,000, depending primarily on the location and number of bedrooms. Vacant land for development is scarcely available. Working-class neighbourhoods include Abrepo, Ahinsan, Suame, Odumase, Manhyia, Asuoyeboa, Bohyen, Kwadaso, Oforikrom, Ayigya, Adukrom, Asawase, Old Kaase, Breman, Ayigya, Denkyemuoso and Bompata. Land values range between US$ 20,000 and US$ 50,000 per acre. Rental values per month for a two- to four-bedroom residential unit range between US$ 70 and US$ 200.

The Low-end market includes Old Tafo, Atonsu, Nyanyano, Moshie Zongo, Aboabo, Behinase, Adwaase, Aburaso and Akyeremade. Land values are the least expensive, between US$ 15,000 and US$ 30,000 per acre. This submarket is characterised by residential units of compound types with shared amenities where a single room is let at an average monthly rent of between US$ 10 and US$ 30, payable in local currency. A typical single room is of an average size of 12.25 square metres.

In Sekondi-Takoradi, the Upmarket residential market includes Beach Road, Airport Ridge and Chapel Hill. The market is largely dominated by expatriates whose preferences are townhouses and gated communities. Rents average between US$ 1,000 and US$ 3,000 per month for average residential space of 230 square metres. The Working-class neighbourhoods include Anaji, Lagos Town, Tanokrom, Fijai Hills, Butumagyebu and Adiembra. Rental values are in the equivalent of US$ 100 per month for a self-contained house of between two and four bedrooms. Unique properties of excellent immediate vicinities and high-quality constructional details attract relatively higher rental values of US$ 200 per month for three or four bedrooms. The submarket is also highly characterised by owner-occupied houses. The low-end market covers neighbourhoods including Essikado, Ketan, Kojokrom, New Takoradi, Kweikuma and Effiakuma, which feature single-room accommodations with shared amenities such as kitchens, bathrooms and sanitary areas. Rental values are very low, up to US$ 25 per month.

The real estate market in Koforidua is principally dominated by residential with a relatively small stock of office, retail and industrial submarkets. Residential units are predominantly single-family detached and multiple-tenant compound houses. Sale prices of two- to four-bedroom properties range between US$ 35,000 and US$ 100,000, with location and quality of finishes as the main determinants. Apartments with similar bedrooms are priced between US$ 20,000 and US$ 45,000. Rental values are between US$ 60 and US$ 100 per month for two to three bedrooms, with rent payable in local currency.

4.3 Office market

The supply of office space in Accra is concentrated in the Central Business District and is dominated by financial institutions and government ministries, departments and agencies. The Ridge neighbourhood and Airport City are fast becoming the prominent business hubs in the city with high-quality stock for multinational institutions and many others. These are Grade A offices that are most attractive and prestigious, typically with a minimum ceiling height of 2.7 metres or more and commanding the highest rent in the country. Grade A office space offers greater floor load capacity that allows greater density of occupancy. Grade B offices, though similar structurally to Grade A, command discounted rents. These are in less desirable locations and have less desirable amenities. Purpose-built Grade A and Grade B offices are estimated to be in excess of 540,000 square metres (m^2). Typical among them are Grade A stock such as Standard Chartered Bank head office (12,049 m^2), Stanbic Heights (20,118 m^2), The

Octagon (36,000 m^2), Ecobank head office (22,000 m^2) and the Accra Financial Centre (14,648 m^2).

Recent developments in Accra, including SCB Tower, Atlantic Tower, SU Tower and 335 Place, as well as TDC Towers in Tema, have increased the office stock to make supply outstrip demand. Rents, however, remain fairly stable despite the increasing supply. Occupier demand averages between 60 square metres and 200 square metres. There is an emerging trend of high demand for serviced office space – fully furnished and fitted. This trend comes with an added advantage of alleviating the burden of huge capital outlay for office setup. There are also a substantial number of Grade B properties on the market, which are mainly government buildings such as SNNIT Emporium and the Ministry of Defence headquarters.

Monthly rent for Grade A office in Accra is between US$ 30 and US$ 45 per square metre, whilst Grade B offices command between US$ 15 and US$ 30 per square metre. Rents are usually paid quarterly in advance. Pipeline developments are estimated to be in excess of 35,000 square metres. Gross yields range between 8 percent and 13 percent, whilst vacancy rates are between 10 percent and 25 percent in Accra. The stock of other office space close to functional obsolescence and substantially older, with very basic facilities and services, are not covered. Office space in Kumasi attracts monthly rent of between US$ 10 per square metre and US$ 20 per square metre, depending on constructional details and location. The proximity of an office building to other businesses is an advantage and has an impact on demand. Demand for offices is high for buildings that accommodate several modes of transportation and have easy access and parking.

The image or reputation of the building is an additional premium to attract high demand. The other demand factor is the tenant mix, which includes the type of business or trade, because tenants' reputations tend to affect each other. In the office market, supply refers to both the quantity of occupied and unoccupied space available at a given time. Demand, in contrast, refers to the sum of occupied space and vacancy that is expected when market rents are stable. The supply and demand factors are essential in rent determination. When supply is less than demand, it is termed a landlord's market, and rent may increase when there is less competition for tenants. In contrast, when supply exceeds demand, it is a tenant's market, with increased competition for tenants. Rents may dip to result in slow lease transactions.

In Takoradi, there are a few Grade B office properties such as the Shippers Council Building, located at Chapel Hill Road. It provides approximately 1,200 square metres and attracts monthly rent of between US$ 8 and US$ 15 per square metre. Other prominent Grade B offices include the Zen Building, a new four-storey building of 360 square metres, and the Baj Freight Building, approximately 650 square metres. Offices are generally owner-occupied in Koforidua. Few built-to-let offices around the post office, central hospital and the market square are, however, available at rental values lower than the range for Takoradi.

4.4 Retail market

Tagged as Africa's new 'bright spot,' the retail market in Ghana was ranked first in Africa and fourth globally by Kearney's Global Retail Development Index (GRDI) in 2019. The Index focuses on market attractiveness, business risk, number of large cities, business efficiency, market saturation, retail sales per capita and country risk. Urbanisation, public investment and foreign direct investment are the principal driving forces.

The last decade has seen an emergence of Western-styled shopping centres or malls in cities such as Accra, Kumasi and Takoradi that characterise retail market growth. Typically, a shopping mall is a group of commercial stores developed, owned and managed as a going concern or entity. Its major feature is an on-site parking with a capacity determined by the size of the mall. A shopping mall also presents multiple rows of stores separated by walkways but enclosed for climate control.

This submarket presents an excellent avenue for retailers to reach shoppers. Some retailers such as Melcom and Citydia have resorted to alternative retail outlets in the secondary market. Properties are let, refurbished and converted from other uses to commercial and serve as stand-alone retail facilities. Established strip centres or small community shops offering low-income consumers value-for-money goods exist in some neighbourhoods in Accra and other urban centres, usually in a straight row, L-shaped or U-shaped with a row of stores facing a parking lot. The centres are distinguished with open canopies on the frontage of the shops and often not with walkways, as they abut parking spaces.

Demand for retail space in shopping malls is expected to surge. Though informal retailing dominates, the recent trend is inclined towards the formal sector. Accra has an estimated 131,405 m^2 of Western-style retail space. The Accra Mall, commissioned in 2008, is the first retail outlet in the country with a total space of 20,000 m^2. Anchor tenants pay between US$ 400 and US$ 600 per square metre per annum, whilst line shops attract less than US$ 950 per square metre per annum. New additions to the stock include the Junction Mall (11,511 m^2) and West Hills Mall – as the largest in West Africa (27,000 m^2).

Vacancy rates range between 20 percent and 50 percent, depending on location and popularity. Prime yields are in the range of 9 percent to 12 percent. In general, rents range between US$ 35 and US$ 80 per square metre per month, payable one year in advance, but could drop to half yearly or quarterly. Retail spaces measuring between 50 square metres and 80 square metres attract the most enquiries. As supply of retail space gradually outstrips effective demand, a number of proposed mall developments may remain on the drawing board until market dynamics improve. Average rents for between 50 square metres and 80 square metres in the secondary retail market range between US$ 8.50 per square metre per month and US$ 35 per square metre per month.

In Kumasi, retail predominates in the Central Business District of Adum. The Kumasi City Mall at Asokwa provides 18,500 square metres of retail space with Shoprite and Game as the anchor tenants. Commissioned in May 2017, the Kumasi City Mall compares favourably to the Accra Mall and the West Hills Mall in Accra. It offers a huge potential for a future 10,000-square-metre expansion. Land values in the city for retail development range between US$ 1 million and US$ 2.5 million per acre, depending on the leasehold term. Retail space commands an average monthly rent of between US$ 10 per square metre and US$ 20 per square metre.

The retail market in Takoradi is made up predominantly of strip centres with the exception of the Takoradi Mall, measuring 11,491 square metres, which was officially commissioned in December 2018. It offers an opportunity for 9,000 square metres of future expansion. Shopping and warehousing facilities command monthly rent of between US$ 12 and US$ 18 per square metre. The retail submarket in Koforidua is largely strip centres, strategically dotted around the central market and along some principal roads.

Shopping malls are characterised by the anchor or major tenant(s). These anchor tenants occupy a large space in a preferred location and also determine the leasing of the rest of the retail space. Tenants are widely differentiated; for instance, some are classified by merchandise type – soft goods, hard goods and GAFO (General merchandise, Apparel, Furniture and Other). Others are categorised on the basis of the size of the retail space they occupy, price lines, image, customer draw and operational requirements. Leasing to an anchor tenant is prioritised in creating a tenant mix, which sets the tone for subsequent lettings. Anchor tenants attract most of the traffic and also determine quality of customers to the shopping mall.

4.5 Industrial market

The industrial market remains the smallest in size relative to the other submarkets. Characteristics of the market include high traffic flow, limited areas of public open space, large buildings with storage facilities, movements of heavy vehicles, on-street and off-street parking, and higher noise levels. The dynamics of the submarket have changed in the last two or three decades with a strong expression of a mixture of industrial, office, retail, warehousing and residential uses. Retail activities are largely associated with industrial zones but in the case of Ghana, the former is overtaking the latter. Warehousing as an ancillary use has always been a key feature of the industrial submarket.

A slow developmental phase has been experienced in Accra with industrial activities limited to three long-established corridors – the North Industrial Area, South Industrial Area and Motorway Industrial Area (popularly known as Spintex Road Industrial Area). Land values in the Cedi equivalent range from US$ 600,000 per acre at Motorway Industrial Area and US$ 1 million per acre for the South Industrial Area to US$ 1.2 million per acre for the North Industrial Area. Nascent submarkets in the last decade can be located along major roads in the residential neighbourhoods of Adenta, Oyibi, Weija, Kuntuse and Oyarifa for light industrial activities where land values average US$ 100,000 per acre. Whilst owner-occupied industrial properties largely exist, demand for space ranging between 300 square metres and 3,500 square metres by local and multinational investors is not uncommon in Accra.

New factories have since 2017 emerged and at various stages of completion nationwide in response to the government's flagship project of One-District-One-Factory (1D1F). This initiative is a big boost in the transformation from an agrarian based economy to an industrialised nation. Rentals for industrial units in general, are at the lowest; pegged averagely at US$ 15 per square metre per month and gross yields between 10 percent and 12 percent. The Kaase, Suame, Asokwa and Asokore Mampong Industrial Areas are prominent in Kumasi where land values range between US$ 600,000 and US$ 800,000 per acre.

A decline in the oil and gas activities of the industrial market in Sekondi-Takoradi has resulted in demand dip for industrial space. A similar trend occurred when the oil sector experienced a boom between 2008 and 2010, which resulted in a sharp decline in the operations of the traditional timber and cocoa industries. Industrial areas in Sekondi-Takoradi include the Takoradi Port area, Effiakuma Shell Road to Sekondi, Airport area, Takoradi-Agona-Tarkwa Road, Aboadze enclave and Sekondi Free Zones. Industries within these enclaves include Olam, Lloyds British, Safebond, Wamco, ETG Ghana, GHUMCO, Weatherford, Baker Hughes, GNPC and Tullow. Land values range between US$ 50,000 and US$ 80,000 per acre. Average rent is US$ 10 per square metre per month. In Koforidua, the industrial submarket is very small and prominent along the Koforidua–Suhum road, and the corridor of Koforidua to Okorase.

Tema was carefully planned as an industrial market development to be an industrial city for the country. In 1951, the government, as part of its development plan, envisioned the Volta River Project to harness the Volta River for hydroelectric power to provide energy for its aluminum smelters. This vision led to the construction of the Akosombo Dam and a deep seaport at Tema to exploit and export mineral resources, specifically bauxite deposits in the Eastern Region. Tema was therefore intended to be the industrial hub in the country and expected to promote a synergy with Accra.

Additionally, the plan included the creation of a township, a 'new town' to provide accommodation for the various workers of these economic activities. The 'new town' was the first of its kind in West Africa at the time. It was characterised by a well-planned scheme that was designed to integrate all advantages of a modern city. Details of the scheme included neighbourhoods for industrial and residential with ancillary uses such as hospitals, social and cultural services, open spaces, schools, markets and community centers as well as a central sewage system.

In this regard, the government, by using the Land Ordinance (No. 38 of 1952), compulsorily acquired about 63 square metres (40,320 acres) of land in 1952, which was subsequently transferred to TDC Company Limited under a lease arrangement for 125 years. TDC has since had the sole responsibility of developing and managing Tema township. This land area, known as the Tema Acquisition Area (TAA), was acquired from three customary authorities, namely Tema (52 percent), Nungua (18 percent) and Kpone (30 percent). In July 1961, Doxiadis and Associates of Greece was entrusted with the preparation of a master plan for the TAA as well as a detailed program for the development of the town and its industrial area for the ensuing 25 years to accommodate 250,000 inhabitants. The master plan made provision for four main zones which included industrial, residential, central business district (CBD) and harbour areas.

The industrial zone developed along the eastern boundaries included the smelter area of the TAA and covered an area of approximately 2,800 acres. Although the idea was to have a mix of both private and publicly owned industries setting up in Tema, most of the earlier industries that were established were mostly large scale, state-owned, capital-intensive manufacturing industries. This was mostly due to the slow pace in the development of the infrastructure network. The completion of four key infrastructure – most of the required infrastructure for industries to function effectively, Harbour in 1961, Tema Oil Refinery in 1963 and the Volta Aluminum Company in 1963 – nonetheless accounted for the industrial boom in early 1963. The main pioneer industries that were sited at the zone ranged from motor assembly plant (UAC Assembling plant that assembled Bedford lorries) to chemical factories, a cement factory, a suitcase and mattress factory (Gaisie West Africa), factories for manufacturing various metals products, textile factories, a fish cold storage plant and a building yard.

The Tema industrial enclave has a total land size of approximately 10,000 acres (40,468,564 square metres), which makes up about a quarter (25 percent) of the total land area of TAA. It is subdivided into three zones – light, heavy and agro-industrial areas. The light industrial area is sparsely distributed along both sides of the National Highway (N1) which passes through TAA and constitutes 13 percent of the total land size. It has enterprises including auto mechanic shops, metal fabrication workshops, furniture workshops, sachet water production and petroleum filling stations. Land values average the Cedi equivalent of US$ 150,000 per acre. The heavy industrial zone with the largest size (73 percent) is located on the eastern corridor of the city and is separated from the residential zone by a linear greenbelt which runs along the main Tema harbour road. The siting of the heavy industrial area on the east of the residential zone and the provision of the greenbelt was to improve the air quality in the residential area by screening to prevent harmful pollutants emanating from the industrial zone. It was also to allow smells and noise to drift harmlessly away from the open land on the north and east of the city. This zone accommodates companies including the Cocoa Processing Company, Nestlé, Bel-Aqua, Tema Steel, Amani Manufacturing, GRIDCO, Tropical Cable and GHACEM. It commands an average land value of US$ 325,000 per acre.

The residue of 14 percent of the industrial zone is the Agro-Industrial Area located at Kpone that abuts the heavy industrial area. This is the location where raw agricultural materials are converted into value-added products in addition to generating income and contributing to the overall economic development of the country. An acreage value of land is between US$ 200,000 and US$ 300,000. The industrial area boasts of good accessibility – road and railway – which links the zone to the residential areas and the harbour. There is the main arterial road that provides easy access to the N1, which is the West African Highway linking Ghana with the Ivory Coast in the west and Nigeria in the east, with Togo and Benin in between. In addition, a 70-kilometre railway network to link the zone to Akosombo is under construction. A waste treatment plant, electricity, good telecommunication network and pipe-borne water are available.

Land-use control and efficient urban management are the two critical tools needed to ensure that the characteristics of real estate submarkets are not compromised in the country. Office, retail and industrial submarkets are relatively small, with few sale transactions and marginal movement in prices. The residential market presents a wide range of upmarket, emerging upmarket, gated, working-class and low-end rental properties. Accra continues to be the single largest residential market for the upmarket and gated communities.

4.6 Mortgage market

Mortgage finance was first introduced in the country with the formation of the First Ghana Building Society (FGBS) in June 1956. Its aim was primarily to encourage individual savings by offering attractive interest rates to accumulate funds for residential development. However, FGBS could not be sustained due to three reasons:

1 General low level of personal incomes.
2 Unattractive interest rates payable by FGBS.
3 Absence of a savings habit among the general public.

An attempt was made in 2004 to resurrect FGBS and make use of new economic and technological advances for its competitiveness. FGBS got licensed to become a Savings and Loans Company, with the National Investment Bank Limited and the Ministry of Finance as the majority shareholders. Its corporate business covered deposit investments, deposit accounts, money transfers and loans. Housing microfinance loans and mortgage loans predominated. An applicant who had operated an account for at least six months and with a minimum deposit of 20 percent of the loan qualified for a mortgage loan to purchase serviced residential plots, purchase or build a house or complete an ongoing residential property. The microfinance scheme was designed to meet the needs of civil servants, public servants, individuals and families working with corporate institutions.

In the 1990s, two other building societies – the Afit Building Society and Reliance Building Society – emerged as private initiatives. Both societies operated in line with FGBS but failed to make significant impact in the mortgage market and have since collapsed. Even the Bank for Housing and Construction (BHC) that was specifically established in 1982 for the real estate and construction sector had its own challenges in promoting the mortgage market. The acceptance of short-term funds from customers to finance mortgage loans greatly accounted for the collapse of BHC. The mortgage market was in its moribund state when the government, through the support of development partners, established the Home Finance Company (HFC) in 1991. Its primary objective was to mobilise and manage long-term funds for the purposes of establishing a sustainable housing finance system in Ghana.

In 1994, HFC metamorphosed into HFC Bank (Gh.) Ltd, and subsequently in 2003 was licensed by the Bank of Ghana as a universal bank. In April 2018, HFC Bank (Gh.) Ltd rebranded as Republic Bank, a subsidiary of Republic Financial Holdings Limited of Trinidad and Tobago. HFC loan repayment was 25 percent of borrower's income over a maximum of 20 years, at 4.5 percent per annum for loans up to the Cedi equivalent of US$ 8,700. Loans in excess of this amount attracted an interest of 6 percent per annum. The Republic Bank continues to be one of the key players in housing financing. Its mortgage portfolio covers home equity, home improvement, home purchase, home completion and home scheme. Indeed, the Republic Bank (Gh.) Ltd and GHL Bank Limited started purely as mortgage banks.

The GHL Bank Ltd was the leading financial institution in residential mortgages in the country until its restructuring in 2017 into a universal bank. It was wholly devoted to mortgages as Ghana Home Loans that was established in 2006. In May 2020, First National Bank acquired GHL Bank Ltd and took over its portfolio of mortgage loans, the biggest in the country at the time, with products range of home purchase (first-time buyers), home construction, home completion, land purchase, home refinance and home owners' equity release – ways to use your house as a means to create additional wealth.

Home Mortgage Finance Act, 2008 (Act 770) regulates home mortgage financing and related matters, including foreclosures in Ghana. It is nonetheless very difficult to recover properties from defaulting customers due to delays in securing foreclosures in the courts, a big restraining force in the mortgage market. An amendment of Act 770 is required to provide simple and unambiguous interpretation and application. Such an intervention will support claims by Teye *et al.*, (2015) that the government needs to ensure that a better loan pricing and repayment mechanism prevails to promote the mortgage market.

A loan that uses real estate as collateral can be referred to as a mortgage. In the primary market, a potential borrower applies for a loan from a bank as the lender. The latter evaluates the borrower's application and decides whether to grant a loan and on what terms or otherwise. The lender will require additional assurance that the loan will be repaid, either through a down payment or mortgage security or a combination of the two. When a loan is concluded, the borrower becomes the mortgagor with the property as the security for repayment and the lender as mortgagee. A mortgage must highlight four characteristics – amount of the loan (principal), interest rate, term of the loan (number of years or months) and frequency of loan repayment (monthly installments or lump sum). The primary mortgage market is underdeveloped in the country and distinguished by limited accessibility, possibly due to the high cost of finance and lack of access to long-term funds. A secondary mortgage market, which ought to provide a vehicle for buying and selling mortgages that have been originated in the primary market, is virtually nonexistent.

Mortgages are normally contracted as long-term transactions, for 30 years and beyond in some developed economies, as against the practice in Ghana where the period ranges from 10 to 25 years. It needs to be stressed that mortgage funding was meant to be a long-term liability procured from long-term sources such as pension funds and insurance companies. Certainly, there is a mismatch in Ghana where such funds are sourced from universal banks whose liabilities are short-term in nature. Though very small in stock, a number of real estate assets in cities across the country have been acquired through mortgage financing. Banks' mortgage requirements vary, but include a recent valuation of the subject property. The valuation provides the basis to estimate a loan-to-value ratio and an interest-cover ratio to aid in establishing the potential default risk.

The option to lend either in local currency (Cedis) or foreign denomination – US$ or UK pound – is the prerogative of the mortgagee, but subject to Bank of Ghana guidelines. Repayment is strictly linked to borrower's income, typically at a repayment to loan ratio of up to 40 percent. Thus, monthly repayment is capped at 40 percent of the mortgagor's monthly income, with high interest rates at between 20 percent and 25 percent for Cedi-denominated loans and 11.5 percent to 12.75 percent for dollar-indexed loans.

Ghana's mortgage market remains underdeveloped, with challenges such as a weak regulatory regime, high capital cost and limited access to long-term funds. The recent establishment of the National Housing and Mortgage Fund (NHMF) by government will provide affordable local currency mortgages and construction finance to developers. It is being piloted through Stanbic Bank, Republic Bank and GCB Bank to provide affordable housing finance to public sector workers using purely local developers; its sustainability is however, a great concern. The establishment of Real Estate Investment Trusts (REITs) in Ghana is at its formative stages following the issuance of guidelines by the Securities and Exchange Commission (SEC). It is expected that REITs will mobilise capital for the real estate market and improve liquidity.

Note

1 The source of all population figures is the Ghana Statistical Service (2010).

References

Anim-Odame, W. (2009). *Residential real estate investment in emerging economies: The case of Ghana*. Unpublished PhD Thesis, Cass Business School, Faculty of Finance, City University, London.

Broll Ghana. (2018). Property market barometer.

Broll Ghana. (2019). Residential market snapshot.

Doxiadis Associates. (1961). Tema: Master programme and plan. *Preliminary Report 4, Document Dox-GHA*, 18, p. 6.

Ghana Statistical Service. (2010). *Population and housing census data analysis report*. Accra: Ghana Statistical Service.

Hilling, D. (1966). Tema: The geography of a port. *Geography*, 51, pp. 111–125.

Home Mortgage Finance Act, 2008 (Act 770), Ghana.

Institute of Real Estate Management of the National Association of Realtors. (2015a). *Marketing and leasing: Office buildings*. Chicago, IL: Institute of Real Estate Management of the National Association of Realtors.

Institute of Real Estate Management of the National Association of Realtors. (2015b). *Marketing and leasing: Retail*. Chicago, IL: Institute of Real Estate Management of the National Association of Realtors.

Jones Lang LaSalle. (2018). Global real estate transparency index. *Global Research*.

Kearney's Global Retail Development Index. (2019).

Keith, J. (1961). *Ghana's Newtown and harbour*. Tema Development Secretariat, Ministry of Information, Accra in association with Neman Neame Limited, Tema.

Kircherr, E. (1968). The evolution of a planned city in West Africa. *Urban Studies*, 5 (2), pp. 207–217.

Ministry of Local Government. (1990). *Planning standards and development guidelines*. Accra: Ministry of Local Government.

Ministry of Water Resources, Works and Housing. (2015). *National housing policy*. Accra: Ministry of Water Resources, Works and Housing.

Owusu-Ansah, A., Soyeh, K. and Asabere, P. (2019). Developer constraints on housing supply in urban Ghana. *International Journal of Housing Markets and Analysis*, 12 (1), pp. 59–73.

Tema Development Corporation. (2004). *Annual report and financial statements*. Tema: Tema Development Corporation.

Tema Development Corporation Legislative Instrument, L.I. 469. (1969). *As amended by L.I. 1468 of 1989*. Tema: Tema Development Corporation.

Teye, J., Teye, I. and Asiedu, M. (2015). Financing housing in Ghana: Challenges to the development of formal mortgage system. *Journal of Housing and the Built Environment*, 30, pp. 1–16.

5 Investment potentials

5.1 Introduction

The performance of real estate investment in Ghana is cyclical in response to the economy. An investment in real estate is generally influenced by inflation hedge potentials. Real estate cash flow is a blend of the characteristics of bond and equity. The investment risk is therefore expected to sit between those for bond and equity. The uniqueness of real estate is manifested in its fixity, permanence, market segmentation, risk, longevity, poor liquidity, large capital requirements and the necessity for management.

Real estate is fixed in location and its fixity defines the scope of its marketability, which is more often limited. It has a permanence characteristic that prescribes its behaviour as a long-term investment vehicle. Its market segmentation permits the treatment of submarkets such as residential, retail, office and industrial. Each of these submarkets is also unique and requires that investors will demonstrate good knowledge of the market dynamics, seek expert advice and rely on performance indicators from the market to achieve optimum return-risk trade-off.

As with all other asset classes, there is an element of risk associated with real estate investment that reflects the market uncertainties due to local, regional, national or international factors or a combination of two or more of these. It may be easy to purchase a property but often, it could be difficult to sell, particularly in emerging markets such as Ghana. Marketability may be slow in comparison with bonds and equity. Real estate acquisition, maintenance and holding tend to necessitate relatively huge sums of money. The large capital requirement makes investors rely on debt finance, though equity sometimes tend to be the reliable and available option, as in Ghana for residential investment.

Prudent estate management is essential to make investments successful. Professional managers should be engaged to deal with lettings, sales, customer relations, property maintenance, taxes and reporting. The cyclical nature of real estate investment performance is driven by the cause-and-effect relationship of supply and demand. A real estate cycle is typically of market expansion that eventually peaks at a point only to be contracted for a period and subsequently achieving another expansion over time.

There is no central 'trading floor' in the market. It lacks flow of information on transactions despite the growing use of technology. Even if a central location existed for transactions, the low liquidity and high heterogeneity of real estate will make it unlikely that transaction flows alone can provide a reliable and consistent picture of the market. Often, information that is available to either principal or intermediary players in the market could commonly be regarded as commercially sensitive and thus a critical challenge to information sharing. The establishment of a real estate performance measurement system must be seen as the primary foundation to generate credible data from the most comprehensive and accurate sources. The credibility and high-quality data, rigour in performance measurement and objectivity in results interpretation are the cornerstone for real estate investment markets.

5.2 Performance measurement

Globalisation of all forms of real estate investment has increasingly demanded that performance benchmarks of high quality and international standards be made accessible to investors and fund managers. In mature real estate markets, performance measurement systems are operated by market intermediaries such as the Investment Property Databank (IPD, UK-based), PCA in Australia, KTI in Finland and NCREIF in US. With the exception of IPD, which is a commercial provider, all others are based on industry associations. Within Europe, UK has shown the richest experience in the construction of real estate performance indices. Some of the indices have been well-established since the 1970s and have also been met by a wide range of competing indices constructed by actuaries and non-real estate specialists such as Combined Actuarial Performance Services (CAPS). Indices constructed by IPD are valuation-based on market value principle and cover standing investments – completed and lettable properties – but exclude their financial performance at the time of their being purchased, sold or in the course of development. The import of this approach was to ensure that the indices only reflect market returns and were not determined by abnormal losses or profits.

There are no data sources in Ghana that would support the construction of a valuation-based real estate index. Though the rented residential market is relatively large, accounting for 31 percent of all households, and 29 percent, marginally smaller in Accra, investments in the residential stock by institutional investors and other large owners likely to conduct recurrent valuations are marginal. Large-scale operators in the market have recently focused on the development of commercial real estate units – upmarket residential, offices and retail – for sale to owner occupiers and lettings. Residential investments are predominantly held by small, private buy-to-let investors, with no requirement to conduct recurrent valuations. It is, however, highly possible to track a large number of transactions in this sector.

A novelty in providing technically robust indicators of the residential market performance from the records held by the Ghana Lands Commission has been conducted (see Anim-Odame *et al.*, 2010a). This was achieved through the construction of the first-ever residential price and rent indices for the aggregate and disaggregate markets. Residential price and rent series were developed for the residential market in Ghana from hedonic models for the period 1992 to 2007. These time series were, in turn, used to generate other performance indicators – yields, nominal and real returns – using transaction-based data for Accra and Tema, the dominant markets in the country.

Several empirical approaches have been proposed in the literature for modelling residential pricing. The choice of an appropriate method depends partly on the purpose and partly on the quality of data (Gallimore *et al.*, 1996; Malpezzi, 2003; Lum, 2004; Sirmans *et al.*, 2005). Residential real estate investments, in contrast to office, retail and industrial markets are internationally and generally measured by valuation-based indices. They carry the general advantage of larger volumes of transactions evidence and relatively homogenous building characteristics, so that performance indices can be constructed from sales and lettings evidence. Data limitation is thus a problem in residential market analysis only when more than an annual frequency is required for the index (Case and Wachter, 2003; Sirmans *et al.*, 2005).

Residential real estate is an asset for which prices can be regarded as a composite of three main sets of factors: the physical attributes of individual properties; location characteristics of the areas in which they sit; and legal structure of their ownership and occupation (Malpezzi, 2003).

Physical features of real estate are in turn a bundle of attributes including the type of structure (detached, semidetached or flat), size as measured by plot size, floor area, number of bedrooms, number of bathrooms, presence of garage and outhouse, number of storeys, age, decoration and structural condition. A set of location characteristics includes travel times to the main employment sectors, shopping centres, and the quantity and quality of major amenities such as schools and parks. Real estate is a durable and indivisible asset and its market value is influenced by the legal interests and use rights: freehold or leasehold ownership, nature of occupants and terms of occupational leases in addition to its location.

Pricing of an individual property in the open market is therefore the outcome of a large set of factors: design, orientation and decoration; bundles of rights and interest; and the fixed location. In a combination, these factors generate the unique price and rent for each asset. Since property attributes cannot be separately traded, there is no direct measure of determining individual contributions to prices and rents without recourse to the others.

Buyers and occupiers are also not heterogeneous. Each of them is permitted to put a different value on specific property characteristics. Thus, the 'market price' of a property at any given time may be defined as the highest price at which a willing vendor would find exactly one willing buyer. As there is only one market spot price for any specific property, all other potential buyers are likely to be precluded from buying that property once the transaction is concluded. This market clearing price nonetheless, fluctuates over time, with changes in expectations about future increases in the market prices among potential purchasers, or due to changes in the availability in the market of particular property features.

The value, price or rent of a real estate asset is important for economic and financial developments. Therefore an accurate measurement of its performance is highly desirable for economic analysis, financial analysis and public policy. From an economic perspective, real estate is a major store of individual wealth. The occupancy of property also accounts for a large fraction of household expenditures. Changes in prices are therefore a strong influence on consumer spending and saving decisions, and also affect overall economic performance (Herring and Wachter, 1999, 2002). From a financial perspective, lending institutions rely on estimates of market value to contract mortgages and estimate lending risks (Herring and Wachter, 1999; Mera and Renaud, 2000). From a social policy standpoint, real estate prices determine housing affordability and the access of different social groups to adequate housing, an important public policy goal in all economies. Further, for market participants in real estate investment, real estate price indices are inputs for asset allocation and investment decisions.

Robust and widely accepted real estate price indices provide informed decisions on macroeconomic and housing policies, and may set important price signals for the capital markets. Seeing that real estate gains increasing prominence as an investment medium in emerging economies, the construction of real estate price and rent indices will provide the signals or inputs needed to develop and implement effective government policies on real estate and also achieve efficiency in capital markets. The ensuing sections present the methodology, empirical findings in the earlier research (Anim-Odame, 2009), implications and the relevance for real estate investments in Ghana.

5.3 Transaction-based property indices

Methodology

Time series produced from hedonic models using 3,250 transaction-based data, running from 1992 to 2007, document movements in prices and rents in Accra and Tema, the dominant commercial conurbations in Ghana. In line with international standards, the results from the first-ever Ghanaian experience suggest that the derived price and rent indices reveal cyclical trends showing weak and strong patches.

The log-linear specification suggested by Malpezzi (2003) and represented by the general form below was employed:

$$P = f(S, N, L, C, T) \qquad [1]$$

where;

P = price (substituted by R where rentals are being estimated);
S = structural characteristics;
N = neighbourhood characteristics;
L = location characteristics;
C = contract characteristics that affect rental income; and
T = the time of transaction.

For notational convenience, equation [1] can be rewritten by collapsing the vectors S, N, L, C and T into a larger vector X. Adopting a common semi-logarithmic functional form, equation [1] is reduced to:

$$P = e^{x\beta\varepsilon} \quad [2]$$

So that:

$$\ln P = X\beta + \varepsilon \quad [3]$$

Since β and ε are unknown true parameters, we estimate:

$$\ln P = Xb + e \quad [4]$$

where *b* and *e* are actual estimates.

By the properties of logarithms, the value of an individual characteristic can be estimated, X_1, at a given level of X_1 as:

$$P = e^{xb} \quad [5]$$

The price of X_1, or any other single attribute, varies with the level of X_1, as well as with the level of other X_i. The price and rent of real estate assets therefore are nonlinear.

The price and rent models are therefore represented by the equations:

$$\ln P(x_j) = \beta_0 + \Sigma_{i=1}^{n} \beta_i \ln(x_{ij}) + \Sigma_{k=1}^{n} \beta_k D kj + \varepsilon_j \quad [6]$$

$$\ln R(x_j) = \beta_0 + \Sigma_{i=1}^{n} \beta_i \ln(x_{ij}) + \Sigma_{k=1}^{n} \beta_k D kj + \varepsilon_j \quad [7]$$

where $\ln P(x_i)$ and $\ln R(x_i)$ are the natural logarithm of price and rent, respectively, β_i and β_K are coefficients, $\ln X_{ij}$ are the natural logarithms of continuous independent variables, D_{kj} are time dummies or other discrete variables and ε_j represents random errors. The parameters β_i and β_K are computed using ordinary least squares.

Price and rental models were first estimated for the aggregate market, and then separately for each of the five submarkets studied – Upmarket, Emerging upmarket, Gated, Working-class and Tema market. This was done partly as a test of robustness of the models when the sample was disaggregated, and partly to investigate any variation in the process of price and rent determination in different submarkets. The results from the hedonic models were used to construct the first-ever residential price and rental indices for the overall and disaggregate markets in Ghana, and to briefly discuss the evolution of prices and rental values over time.

The full set of property-specific variables employed cover all primary physical characteristics: *type of unit (single family detached or semidetached), plot size, gross internal floor area, number of bedrooms, number of storeys and the presence or otherwise of garage and outhouse*. Fields for legal and leasing characteristics cover the *freehold ownership* (coded as state or customary owner) and *unexpired term* of underlying leases. A final field classified the *quality of external landscaping*.

Empirical findings

The results in the original US$ denomination for the aggregate market were also analysed at the disaggregate level. All estimations were conducted on the original data converted to Cedis (using a Cedi:US$ exchange rate calculated as the average of monthly rates through the year of transaction) in order to calculate Cedi-denominated price and rent indices for aggregate and disaggregate markets. The recalculation in Cedis raised no additional modelling issues.

As expected, the location variables were all strongly significant, and pointed to a price differentiation between Accra and Tema, and also to the premium prices for Upmarket and Gated submarkets within Accra. The primary real estate characteristics – location, number of storeys, number of bedrooms, the presence of garage and outhouse, detached, good quality of landscaping and plot size variables – were all strongly significant at the 1 percent level with the expected signs as significant price and rent determinants in Ghana. Detached status was also, in all markets, an important price and rent determinant.

The indices for price and rent of residential investments were calculated and constructed from the coefficients on the year dummies. Admittedly, the task was certainly challenging. It proved time-consuming and more laborious than envisaged. A number of potential transactions had to be discarded from the sample size due to missing or unverified information. Nonetheless, the employed final samples represented the most accurate historical record available for the residential market. Beyond the Ghanaian market, the approach suggests that the process of constructing residential indices from records held by state

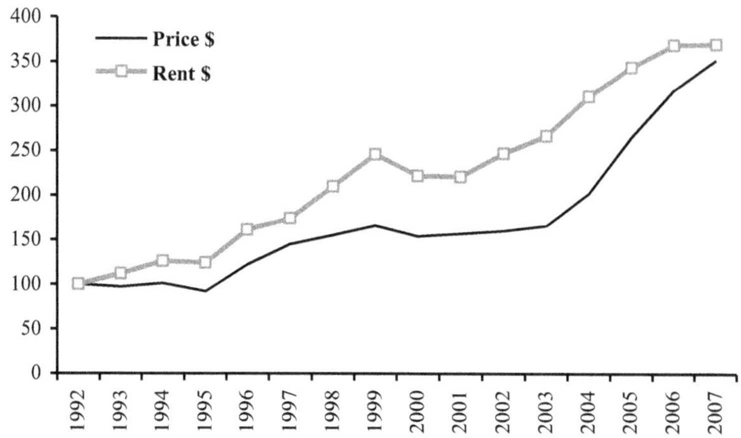

Figure 5.1 Residential price and rent indices US$, 1992 = 100

land registration and taxation authorities may be replicable in other emerging or sub-Sahara African countries where there are similar systems of land registration, provided that the task of data assembly and validation is feasible.

The price index produced in US$ (see Figure 5.1) shows flat or falling prices from 1992 to 1995 followed by a substantial appreciation from the years 1996 to 1999, then a further flat patch in the early 2000s and a final strong surge in prices in the last four years. The strongest single-year rate of dollar price appreciation of 32 percent was in 1996. This may in part be explained by the abolishing of the restrictive law[1] (PNDC Law 150) on letting and acquisition of property by foreign companies. The annualised rate of capital appreciation was 8.8 percent per annum for the 16-year period.

Rents rather rose gradually in the early 1990s, but declined in 1995 and then picked up rapidly from 1996 to a peak in 1999. Through 2000 and 2001 rents fell, followed by a sharp increase from 2002 to 2006, which levelled off in 2007. Overall, an annualised rental growth of 9.1 percent was achieved over the full 16 years, fractionally higher than the dollar-denominated growth in prices of 8.8 percent per annum.

Figure 5.2 shows the price and rent indices expressed in local currency (Cedis). From 1992 to 2007, the Cedi:US$ exchange rate rose from 437 to 9,358, with a depreciation in the value of the Cedi of up to 100 percent in individual years. The profile of residential price changes in Cedis was therefore significantly different from that in US$. There had been a continuous growth in Cedi residential prices throughout the period, at rates ranging from 13 percent to 94 percent per annum. Over the whole period, prices had risen by a factor of 75, an annualised rate of 32.4 percent per annum. As

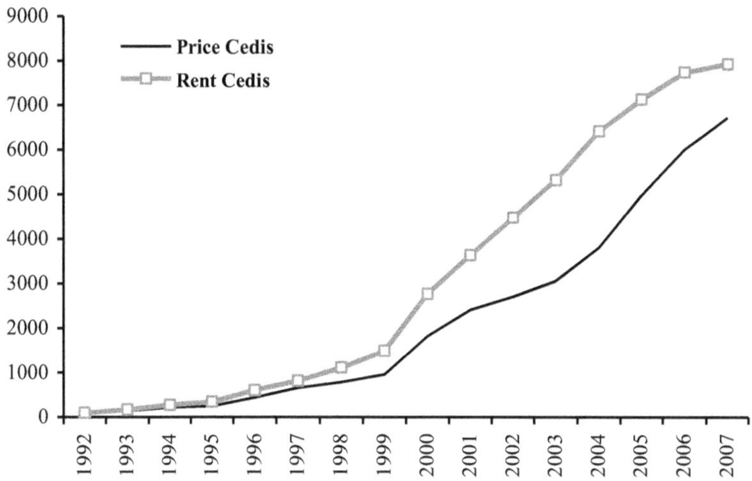

Figure 5.2 Residential price and rent indices Cedis (¢), 1992 = 100

with capital appreciation, in local currency, rents increased every year, with the strongest rise (75 percent) recorded in 1996, again, following the repeal of PNDC Law 150.

The very high nominal rate of capital appreciation should be compared with the high rate of inflation, which had averaged 23 percent per annum over the same period. In real terms, therefore, Cedi-denominated property prices increased at an annualised rate of 8.2 percent per annum. Over the 16 years covered, annualised rental growth had run at 33.8 percent per annum in nominal terms, and 8.6 percent per annum in real terms.

Having established overall price and rent indices from data on the total sample, and through the full time period available, further analysis took the form of tests for robustness for both price and rent models by estimating results for different subsamples of the population of transactions, and then the production of separate models for each submarket. To identify differences in price and rent movements over time for different submarkets, the hedonic price and rental models in US$ for each submarket were regressed separately rather than in a single panel. The recalculation in Cedis raises no additional modelling issues.

Figure 5.3 shows the evolution of rental values in US$ over time in each submarket. The Emerging upmarket and Working-class submarket experienced much high volatility in levels of rents, and higher average growth than the other submarkets. In the case of the Emerging upmarket, some of the high volatility is attributable to the relatively small sample size of observations (97, or 9 percent of the total).

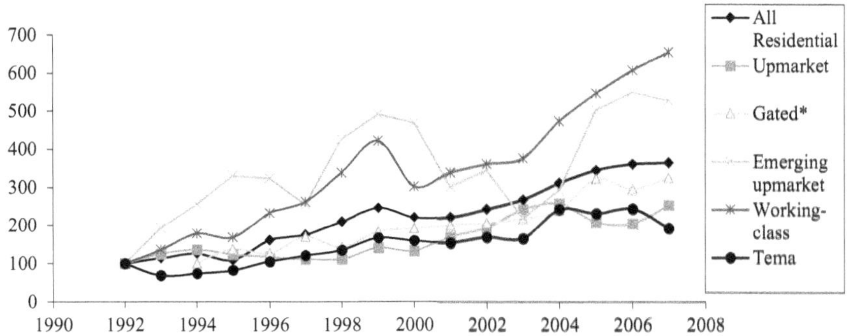

Figure 5.3 Rental value indices by submarkets, US$ 1992 = 100
Note: Gated * 1994 = 100

This was not, however, the case for the Working-class submarket, which had the largest sample of rental observations (382, or 34 percent of the total). In other submarkets, the progression of rental growth has been relatively stable, charting a similar pattern to the aggregate market. On the measure of annual growth rates, the highest correlation between any pair of submarkets is only 0.43 for the Emerging upmarket and the Working-class market, and several pairs were negatively correlated. It did not appear that rental trends in individual submarkets were very strongly integrated with the overall market.

Figure 5.4 plots the growth in transaction prices for residential investments across submarkets in dollar denominations. For comparison, the annualised price growth across submarkets was compared with rental growth rates discussed previously. Long-term price growth ranged from 3.6 percent per annum in Tema to 13.4 percent per annum in the Emerging upmarket. This result is consistent with findings in Antwi and Omirin (2006), which provides price growth of up to 10 percent. The broad pattern across submarkets in rates of price growth was close to that for rates of rental growth – a product of the fairly small variation in yield movements across submarkets. Thus, the only differences in the rank ordering of submarkets by price growth from that by rental growth was for the Emerging upmarket and Working-class submarkets, which were respectively first and second in the ranking by price growth, but switched places in the ranking by rental growth. As was found for rental growth, price growth was stronger and more volatile in the Emerging upmarket and Working-class submarkets than in others (see Figure 5.4).

As shown in Figure 5.5, the profile of reversionary yields over the historic period was fairly flat. For the overall market, the yield averaged 7.9 percent over 16 years of the series, with a range from +0.6 percentage point to −1.0 percentage point around that average.

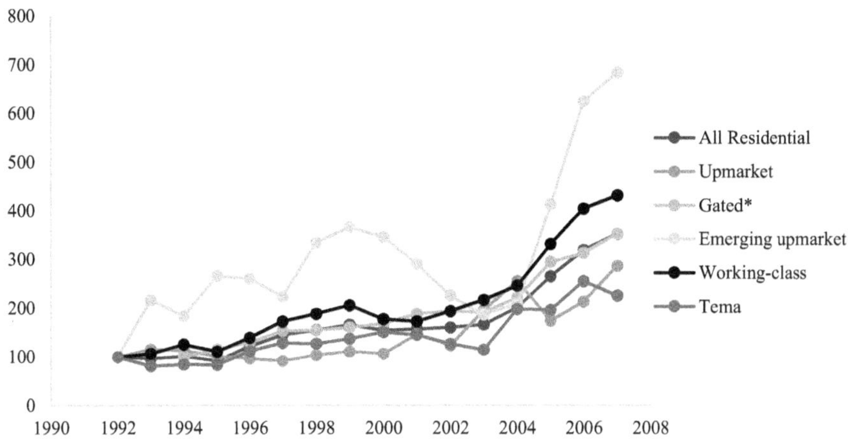

Figure 5.4 Residential price indices by submarkets, US$ 1992 = 100
Note: Gated * 1994 = 100

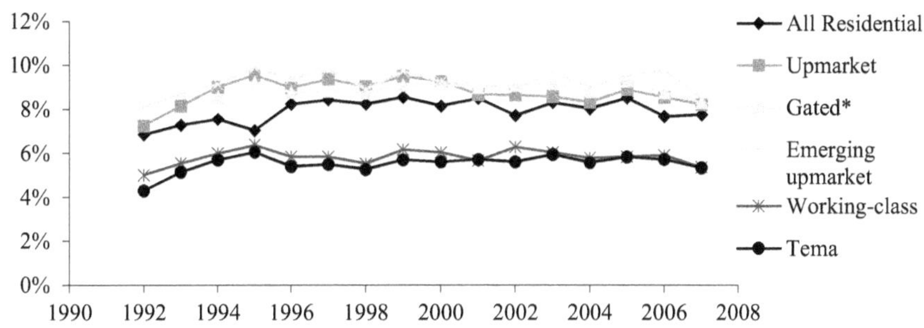

Figure 5.5 Residential reversionary yields by submarkets: 1992–2007
Note: Gated * 1994 = 100

After a steep rise in the level of yield in 1996, there was neither pronounced time trend nor sustained shorter-term direction in yield movements, which seemed to show random fluctuations around a stable average of 8.2 percent from 1996 to 2005. Only the last two years suggested what may be a sustained fall to 2007 figure of 7.7 percent. For a given rent, the fall in yields from 2005 to 2007 would be equivalent to a boost of capital values of around 10 percent.

There appeared to be a strong differentiation across submarkets in long-term rental growth. The Upmarket (6.4 percent) and Tema (4.7 percent) submarkets had seen growth rates well below the average for All Residential (9.1 percent), with above average rates for the Gated (9.5 percent), Emerging upmarket (11.7 percent) and Working-class submarkets (13.4 percent). All Residential (9.3 percent), however, showed standard deviations in annual rental growth rates which were well above their means, running from 15 percent in the Upmarket, Gated (17.2 percent), Working-class (16.7 percent), Tema (16.9 percent) to 37 percent for the Emerging upmarket. Given the limitation to only 16 observations and high levels of variance, none of the differences across submarkets in mean annual growth were statistically significant from the average for All Residential at the 9.1 percent level. Indeed, there were no statistically significant differences between the means for any pair of submarkets.

Any explanation of differences in rental growth across submarkets must, therefore, be qualified by absence of strong statistical significance imposed by the limited number of annual observations. The growth in transaction prices and rental values for residential investments across submarkets in dollar denomination is relevant. For comparison, the annualised price growth across submarkets has been compared with the rental growth.

Long-term price growth runs from 3.6 percent per annum in Tema, Upmarket (7.2 percent), Gated (10.8 percent) and Working-class (11.4 percent) to 13.4 percent per annum in the Emerging upmarket. With 8.7 percent for All Residential, the broad pattern across submarkets in price growth was close to that for rental growth (noted previously) – a product of the fairly small variation in yield movements across submarkets. Thus, the only differences in the rank ordering of submarkets by price growth from that by rental growth was for the Emerging upmarket (11.7 percent) and Working-class (13.4 percent) submarkets, which were respectively first and second in the ranking by price growth but switched places in the ranking by rental growth.

Implications and relevance

The development of rental values over time in the Upmarket was analysed to show that the unadjusted rent series presented a strong rise from 1997 to 2004, and an apparently very steep decline from 2004 to 2007. But the comparison with the hedonically adjusted rent index suggested that part of the long rise was due to a rising average quality of real estate assets traded, so that unadjusted rents rose by 256 percent while after adjustment for quality mix the hedonic rent index rose by 230 percent. After 2004 the unadjusted rent index suggested a massive 36 percent fall in rents, while the hedonic measure showed only a cumulative 2 percent fall. The implication is that recent trading in this area had shifted sharply towards smaller and lower-value units.

Since rents are not only determined by the number of bedrooms, tenants prefer houses that provide bigger floor areas. The results seemed to suggest that, for example, in the Upmarket, Gated and Emerging upmarkets, properties with luxury amenities including study areas, more than one living area, guest rooms, children's rooms and bedrooms with en suite baths are likely to deliver big floor areas to attract premium rent. Similarly, in the Working-class and Tema submarkets, bigger houses with additional rooms such as studies and additional family areas attract higher prices because these could easily be converted into additional bedrooms.

To examine the evolution of values across submarkets and given an indication of the role of changes in quality mix in rental levels, trends in unadjusted average rents per square metre were also compared with hedonically adjusted rents per square metre. The unadjusted rental figures were simple averages of the transactions for each year, and therefore combined the impacts of general market rental levels over time with any changes in the quality mix of properties transacted. The hedonically adjusted figures represented only movements in the general price level, and corrected for changes in quality. Over time, a higher growth in adjusted rents than in unadjusted average, for example, suggested a downward shift in the quality of properties traded, for example, in Upmarket and Tema, and vice versa, for Emerging upmarket and Working-class market. Gated communities nonetheless had produced a fairly consistent quality of residential units.

Figure 5.6 provides a long-term comparison of unadjusted and adjusted rental growth for each submarket over the whole period of the analysis. In Gated communities, Emerging upmarket and Working-class submarkets, the quality mix appeared to have been improving, with adjusted rental growth

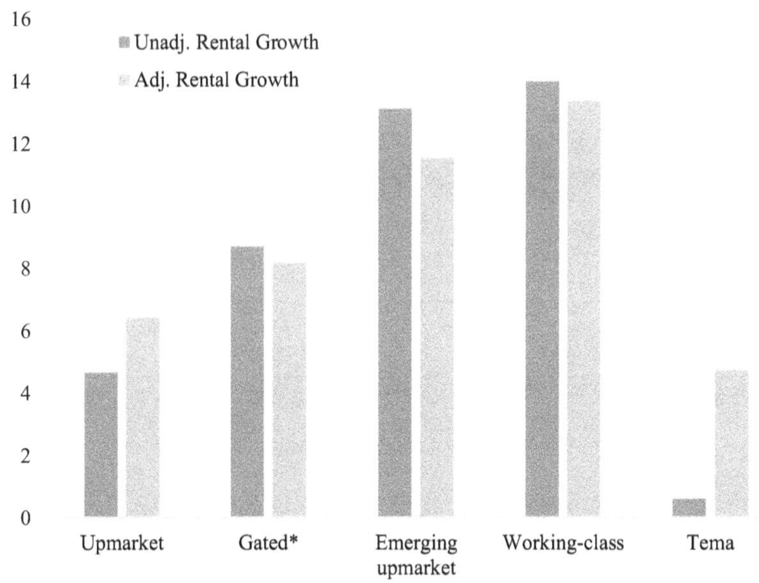

Figure 5.6 Unadjusted and hedonically adjusted rental growths: 1992–2007
Note: Gated ⋆ 1994 = 100

rates significantly below the unadjusted figures. In Upmarket and Tema, the reverse was the case, with the figures suggesting an overall fall in quality. For the Upmarket, it could be attributed to the prevalence of subdivision of large plots into smaller lots for redevelopment, and for Tema, the reduction in quality was likely to reflect the delivery of many houses by TDC Development Company for the Working-class and Low-end submarkets.

Table 5.1 shows the set of variables contributing to total returns over the full period of the analysis. Income returns, reflecting an assumed leasing pattern of evenly spread leases across all submarkets, run 4.9 percent to 7.8 percent below the level of average reversionary yields, which reflects the substantial rental growth which could make the typical portfolio strongly reversionary.

Long-term rates of total return range from 9.7 percent per annum in Tema, Working-class (14.3 percent), Upmarket (14.5 percent) and Gated (16.6 percent) to 20.5 percent per annum in the Emerging upmarket with All Residential at 14.6 percent. As with measures of rental growth and price changes, and despite the substantial spread in returns, none of the differences between submarkets in average rates of return were statistically significant at the 10 percent level. The variation in returns mainly reflected the variation in rates of capital growth, which in turn had been driven mostly by variation in the growth of rental values across submarkets.

The profile of total returns, and rank ordering by returns across submarkets, were slightly different from those for rates of price growth and capital growth. This performance was achieved because the relatively low income return for the Working-class submarket partially offsets above average rates of capital growth, and high income return for the Upmarket partially offsets low capital growth. Tema remained, however, the weakest market ranked by all performance measures relative to submarkets in Accra.

The results also show no consistent trade-off between rates of return and risk across submarkets with the exception of the Emerging upmarket (see

Table 5.1 Residential investment performance by submarkets: 1992–2007, US$ percent pa

	All Residential	*Upmarket*	*Gated*	*Emerging upmarket*	*Working-class*	*Tema*
Average yield %	7.9	8.7	8.9	8.2	5.9	5.7
		Annualised % per annum				
Rental growth	9.1	6.4	9.5	11.7	13.4	4.7
Price growth	8.8	7.3	10.2	13.7	10.2	5.6
Income return	6.7	7.8	7.4	7.0	4.9	5.0
Capital growth	7.7	6.3	9.2	12.6	9.2	4.6
Total return	14.6	14.5	16.6	20.5	14.3	9.7
Risk (SD of return)	11.6	21.9	8.4	39.6	12.2	22.0

Figure 5.7). For All Residential, as seen in Table 5.1, the standard deviation at 11.6 percent per annum is slightly below the mean annual return of 14.6 percent. The Upmarket, Gated and Working-class submarkets showed a spread of risk from 8.4 percent per annum to 21.9 percent per annum for broadly comparable returns of 14.3 percent per annum to 16.6 percent per annum.

The Tema market showed relatively high risk for a below-average rate of return. Again, only the Emerging upmarket shows the combination of high return and high risk normally expected. Most submarkets in Accra and Tema showed a broadly similar profile in total returns over time. For the Upmarket, Gated and Working-class submarkets, returns tracked fairly closely together through the period 1992 to 2007. The most notable exception is the Emerging upmarket, which showed higher rates of return through most of the 1990s and a very strong surge in returns after 2004. The Tema market once again yielded a relative weakening of returns after 2000.

Such real estate performance indicators may be beneficial for policy formulation, particularly for housing affordability and investment decisions. The results demonstrate that hedonic models constructed using transaction-based data achieved high levels of explanation of the variation in real estate prices and rents. Results further suggested that residential values rose substantially from the mid-1990s following the repeal of PNDC Law 150, and again from 2003 to 2007 with flat or falling values in the first half of the 1990s and in the early 2000s. Annualised over the 16 years of the price index, the rise in capital values measured in both US$ and Ghanaian Cedis suggested that investors in

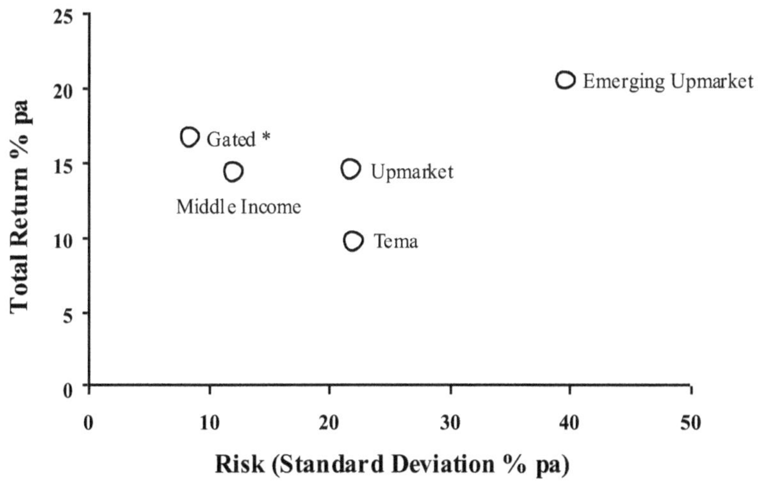

Figure 5.7 Returns and risks by submarkets, US$ percent pa
Gated * 1994 = 100

residential real estate could achieve appreciable capital growth of 9 percent and 32.4 percent, respectively.

It is further demonstrated that econometric tools could be employed to analyse real estate data in emerging markets such as Ghana to show the impact of residential attributes on its price and rent and also test variations in submarkets' performance. This work fills the gaps in the available literature by providing evidence to support the 'debate' that residential real estate markets may be disaggregated on the basis of neighbourhood qualities; the principle of location, location and location thus tested. An inclusion of estimated net investment yields and rental income returns to create measures of total return has provided the basis for an analysis of the performance of residential real estate investments in Ghana relative to other assets, which Chapter 6 presents.

Note

1 The External Companies and Diplomatic Missions (acquisition or rental of immovable property) Law, 1986 (PNDCL 150) established a Committee which performed the functions conferred on it by this Law and in addition ensured the implementation of the provisions thereof. Section 3 of the Law provided that rent payable in respect of any immovable property situated in Ghana under any lease or tenancy agreement granted by any person to a diplomatic mission, consulate, international organisation, external company or an official thereof, or any premium payable in respect of any such property to be let, or the purchase price of any such property where it is sold or assigned to a diplomatic mission, consulate, international organisation, external company or an official thereof, shall be determined and paid in convertible currency. Such rent, premium or purchase price that was determined by the landlord or owner was statutory subject to approval or variation by the Committee. Section 5 provided that any rent, premium or purchase price payable shall be paid through the Ministry of Foreign Affairs by cheque drawn in favour of the Bank of Ghana to the credit of the landlord or owner to whom the rent, premium or purchase price was due. Upon clearance of the cheque, the Bank of Ghana shall pay the Cedi equivalent at the prevailing rate of exchange such part of the amount as the Committee may determine. The remaining part of the amount not paid in Cedis under this Law shall be retained by the Bank of Ghana and paid in convertible currency into a foreign exchange account opened by the landlord or owner to whom the amount is due with any commercial bank approved by the Bank of Ghana. Section 6 of the Law provided that any immovable property to which this Law applies shall be subject to valuation by the Land Valuation Board (government Valuers) for the purpose of ascertaining and determining the rent, premium or purchase price.

References

Anim-Odame, W. (2009). *Residential real estate investment in emerging economies: The case of Ghana*. Unpublished PhD Thesis, Cass Business School, Faculty of Finance, City University, London.

Anim-Odame, W. (2012). The nascent real estate market in Ghana. *Journal of Real Estate Literature*, 20 (2), pp. 289–304.

Anim-Odame, W., Key, K. and Stevenson, S. (2009). Measures of real estate values from land registration and valuation systems in emerging economies: The case of Ghana. *Journal of Real Estate Literature*, 17 (1), pp. 63–84.

Anim-Odame, W., Key, T. and Stevenson, S. (2010a). The Ghanaian transaction-based residential indices. *International Journal for Housing Market and Analysis*, 3 (3), pp. 216–232. Paper was earlier presented at the 9th African Real Estate Society Conference, Lagos, Nigeria, 20–22 October 2009.

Anim-Odame, W., Key, T. and Stevenson, S. (2010b). Residential market development in sub-Saharan Africa. *International Journal for Housing Market and Analysis*, 3 (4), pp. 308–326.

Antwi, A. and Omirin, M. (2006). The investment performance of informal properties in Accra, Ghana and Lagos, Nigeria. *RICS Research Paper Series*, 6 (4).

Armitage, L. (1996). *Constraints to the operation of commercial real estate market in South-East Asia*. London: RICS Research Conference, The Cutting Edge.

Belniak, S. and Schwartz Jr., A. (2000). The nascent Polish real estate market. *Journal of Real Estate Literature*, 8 (1), pp. 19–33.

Broll Ghana. (2018). Property market barometer.

Broll Ghana. (2019). Residential market snapshot.

Case, B. and Wachter, S. (2003). *Residential real estate price indices as financial soundness indicators: Methodological issues*, BIS Papers No. 21. Board of Governors of the Federal Reserve, Ghana.

External Companies and Diplomatic Missions (acquisition or rental of immovable property) Act, 1986 (PNDCL 150), Ghana.

Gallimore, P., Fletcher, M. and Carter, M. (1996). Modelling the influence of location on value, *Journal of Real Estate Valuation and Investment*, 14 (1), pp. 6–19.

Herring, R. and Wachter, S. (1999). *Real estate booms and banking busts – An international perspective*. Washington, DC: Group of Thirty, Occasional Paper 58.

Herring, R. and Wachter, S. (2002). Real estate bubbles. In: G. Kaufman ed., *Asset price bubbles: Implications for monetary, regulatory, and international policies*. Cambridge, MA: MIT Press.

Lum, S. K. (2004). Property price indices in the Commonwealth – Construction methodologies and problems. *Journal of Property Investment and Finance*, 22 (1), pp. 25–54.

Malpezzi, S. (2003). Hedonic pricing models: A selective and applied review. In: K. Gibb and A. O'Sullivan ed., *Housing economics and public policy: Essays in honour of Duncan MacLennan*. London: Blackwell Science.

McGreal, S., Parsa, A. and Keivani, R. (2001). Perceptions of real estate markets in central Europe: A survey of European investors. *Journal of Real Estate Literature*, 9 (2), pp. 145–159.

Mera, K. and Renaud, B. (2000). *Asia's financial crisis and the role of real estate*. New York: M. E. Sharpe Inc.

Sirmans, C. F. and Worzala, E. (2003). International direct real estate investment: A review of the literature. *Urban Studies*, 40, 108–114.

Sirmans, G. S., Macpherson, D. and Zietz, E. (2005). The composition of hedonic pricing models. *Journal of Real Estate Literature*, 13 (1), pp. 3–43.

Sirota, D. (2014). *Essentials of real estate investment*. 10th ed. La Crosse, WI: Dearborn Real Estate Education.

Sirota, D. and Barrell, D. (2010). *Essentials of real estate finance*. 12th ed. La Crosse, WI: Dearborn Real Estate Education.

6 Market competitiveness

6.1 Introduction

Time series have been employed in this chapter to generate nominal and real returns as additional performance indicators for the dominant real estate market in Ghana. The first part presents quantitative and comparative analysis of the market against other investment vehicles in the country. An international perspective of the performance of the residential investment market is analysed in the second part. This approach is intended to provide indicators that form the basis for modelling the causal relationships between real estate market and the economy.

Ghana has since 1992 enjoyed a stable democracy and is widely considered as a regional model for political and economic reforms in sub-Saharan Africa. The quality of its investment climate is defined by the perceived level of corruption in the country. Out of 180 countries considered for the Transparency International Corruption Perception Index 2019, Ghana is ranked 80th with a score of 41, above its African peers such as Nigeria (146th), Tanzania (96th), Kenya (137th) and Uganda (137th). Seychelles (27th), Namibia (56th) and South Africa (70th) nonetheless, outperformed Ghana (Transparency International, 2020).

6.2 Understanding the fundamentals of investment vehicles

There is a huge potential foreign direct investment (FDI) into emerging economies such as Ghana with a possibility that most of these investments would manifest in the real estate market. The volume of international money transferred into Ghana has increased significantly in recent years, in part as a response to the growing real estate market. This viewpoint is accentuated by the massive stock of residential units that have emerged in the well-established prime neighbourhoods of Airport Residential, Cantonments, Labone, Ridge and in the fast- growing neighbourhoods such as East Legon Extension, North Legon and Airport East in Accra and other urban centers.

The contribution of real estate to national economy has been measured by studies using macroeconomic indicators such as GDP (see Hetherington, 1988;

Gardiner and Henneberry, 1988, 1991; Crosby and Keogh, 1990; Liang and Gordon, 2003). Whilst the value of commercial real estate generally is equivalent to 45 percent of GDP in mature developed countries, Hughes and Arissen (2005) estimates the contribution of higher quality real estate at less than 45 percent of GDP for developing countries. A number of countries, including Ghana, in sub-Saharan Africa continues to demonstrate a growing real estate investment markets that offer new investment opportunities. By employing the formula[1] of Hughes and Arissen (2005), the value of investible real estate market in Ghana is assessed at 15.2 percent of GDP.

As far back as 1968, it was envisaged that the establishment of a stock market in Ghana would serve as a significant component of economic development. However, due to an unstable political and economic environment as well as lack of political will, the establishment of a functional stock market was long delayed. It was not until November 1990, when under the Stock Exchange Act, 1971 (Act 384), the first trading of the Ghana Stock Exchange (GSE) was conducted (Ghana Stock Exchange, 2006). Using the index of stock market capitalisation to GDP ratio, Yartey (2006) describes the GSE as not very important in the first four years of its establishment. The stock market capitalisation as a proportion of GDP, however, climbed to 35 percent in 1994, very close to the world average of 38.2 percent. The GSE itself calculates and publishes the GSE All-Shares Index, covering all listed equities. The base for the GSE Index is December 1993, one year later than the base of the performance calculated for residential investments in the country.

To give a full comparison of the local equity market with residential investment, an alternative source of stock market performance has been used, the Databank Index produced for the same period – 1992 to 2007 – by Databank Group. This company tracks the market's performance from 1990, covering all stocks listed on the GSE, and showing annual price changes and dividend yields. As at December 2007, there were 32 GSE-listed companies, with a total market capitalisation of US$ 1.32 billion.

6.3 Benchmarks for comparison

Figure 6.1 presents yields for residential market, equities and treasury bills (T-bills) as well as residential income returns and rates of inflation from 1992 to 2007. Stock market dividend yields were high from 1992 to 1997, when yields escalated to 13 percent. From 1998 to 2002, with a decline in the rate of inflation, yields settled at lower, more stable rates between 6 percent and 7 percent. The period 2004 to 2007 recorded a sharp dip in dividend yields, falling to 2 percent by the end of 2007. Over the period 1992 to 2007, dividend yields averaged at 6 percent. Yields on T-bills had also reflected the downtrend in the rate of inflation, falling from a peak of 43 percent in 1997 to 10 percent in 2006 and 2007. At these levels, T-bills yields were in line with rates of inflation.

Residential yields showed a different trend over time from those of other assets, remaining relatively flat despite the change in the rate of inflation. The

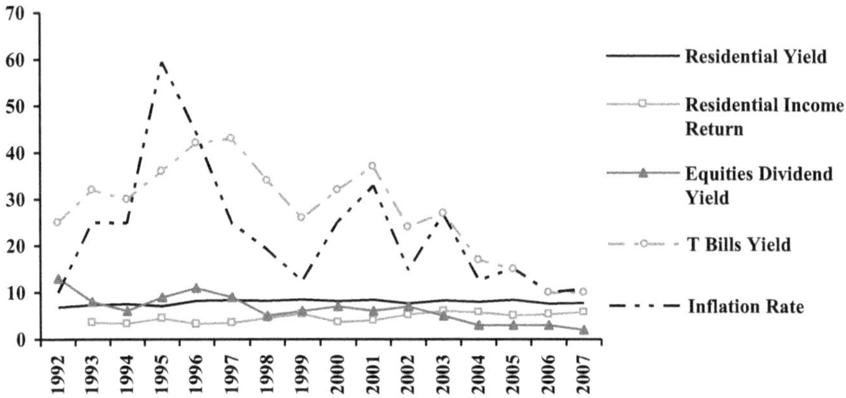

Figure 6.1 Residential, equity, T-bills yields and inflation rates (percent): 1992–2007

reversionary residential yields were close to or below equities dividend yields up to 1997, but ran well above equities yields between 2003 and 2007. The residential yield determination was elevated by the high level of reversions produced by high rates of nominal rental growth, especially in the 1990s. Residential income returns therefore provided a more appropriate comparison with equity dividend and T-bills yields. Rates of income return were well below equity dividend yields up to 2002, but by the end of 2007 had risen to 3.8 percentage points above equities, the largest margin in the history of the series.

Figures 6.2 and 6.3 compare the total returns across Ghanaian asset classes set against the rate of inflation, and Table 6.1 summarises performance over the 16 years.

Over the full period, both returns and risks across the asset classes fall in line with the expectations of investment theory. T-bills, with variation in returns driven solely by interest rate movements, showed the lowest risk and lowest return of the three. Equities, characterised by highly uncertain and variable dividend distributions and capital values, showed the highest return and highest risk. Residential real estate, with a blend of fixed rental incomes determined by leases, and variable incomes on review and relettings determined by rental growth, showed both returns and risks between T-bills and equities. Expressed as a Sharpe Ratio (asset return less T-bills return divided by standard deviation of the asset), the risk adjusted excess returns on residential real estate at 0.49 was marginally above that on equities at 0.45. Against other asset classes in Ghana, therefore, residential real estate had offered a competitive return, commensurate with its risk. Residential investment had also provided more consistent returns than equities (see Figures 6.2 and 6.3). The rate of return on residential investment did not dip below zero in any of the 16-year history, against two for

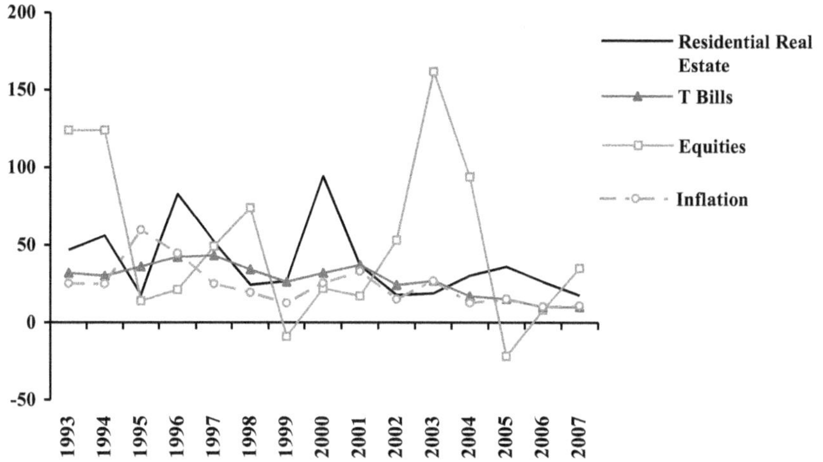

Figure 6.2 Annual total returns by asset class (percent pa) Cedis (¢): 1993–2007

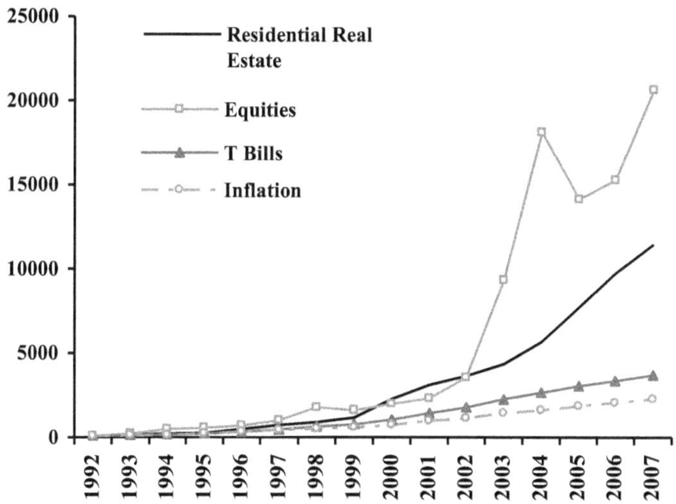

Figure 6.3 Total return indices by asset class, Cedis (¢): 1992 = 100

equities in the same period. Similarly, the annual return on residential investment lagged below inflation in only two out of 16 years, compared to seven years with sub-inflation returns on equities, and five years with sub-inflation returns on T-bills. Again, residential investment produced a return below that of T-bills in five years of the period, compared to seven for equities.

Table 6.1 Ghanaian investments annualised total returns; Cedis percent pa

	Residential real estate	*Equities*	*T-Bills*
	Nominal total return % per annum		
Annualised	37.2	42.7	27.2
mean	38.9	51.1	27.7
Standard deviation	22.9	52.1	10.3

Table 6.2 Correlations in annual returns across asset classes; Cedis

Correlation matrix			
	Residential real estate	*Equities*	*T-Bills*
Residential real estate	1.00		
Equities	–0.08	1.00	
T-bills	0.48	0.12	1.00

Residential markets also offered investors the strong diversification benefits normally associated with assets portfolios (Table 6.2). The correlation between residential real estate and equities was not statistically different from zero, and the correlation with T-bills was moderate at 0.48.

6.4 Comparison of sub-Saharan African markets

In examining selected real estate markets in sub-Saharan Africa – Ghana, Kenya, Nigeria, South Africa, Uganda and Namibia – this section makes an original contribution to the understanding of real estate market potentials and, in particular, presents characteristics to confirm the uniqueness of each market. Real estate markets in sub-Saharan Africa, with the exception of South Africa, share characteristics of emerging markets in terms of limited transaction data, low quality of data, transparency issues, valuation standards and the inactive participation of international market intermediaries.

A large increase in global real estate capital flows has, in the last decade, been a major factor increasing the transparency and information of a set of 'emerging' real estate markets in Africa. The size of higher-quality real estate investment stocks in sub-Saharan African markets, with the exception of South Africa, suggests the markets are well outside the investment horizons of global investors. The evolution of the markets in the subregion is likely to be largely driven by domestic rather than foreign capital flows in the medium term.

Analysis and findings in this section are based on the 2014 Global Real Estate Transparency Index (GRETI) by Jones Lang LaSalle (JLL); the Global Competitiveness Index (GCI), 2015 by the World Economic Forum; the

Global Property Guide, 2015 and Doing Business 2020 Report by the World Bank. GRETI is a unique survey that quantifies real estate market transparency across the globe. It was first published in 1999 and its eighth edition in 2014 studies transparency improvements in 102 real estate markets, 12 of which are in sub-Saharan Africa. The construction of the Index embodies the factors considered important by global real estate investors. GRETI employs a weighted score of subjective ratings by JLL covering five sets of factors: the availability of accurate financial and market fundamentals data, regulatory and legal environment, security and enforceability of real estate ownership rights, financial disclosure and governance of listed real estate companies, and zoning and building regulations.

The competitiveness landscape of 144 economies was assessed by GCI to provide insight into the drivers of their productivity and prosperity. Different aspects of competitiveness have been captured under 12 pillars – institutions, infrastructure, macroeconomic environment, health and primary education, higher education, goods market efficiency, labour market efficiency, financial market development, technology readiness, market size, business sophistication and innovation – and employed in the construction of the Global Competitiveness Index. The 2015 index covers 35 economies in Africa and remains the most comprehensive assessment of competitiveness worldwide.

A platform for the world's best investment opportunities in residential real estate is provided by the Global Property Guide. Its database on global rental yields, transactions costs, vacancy rates and levels of real estate taxes is based on research by an in-house team and employed to analyse investment opportunities in sub-Saharan Africa.

The 2020 Doing Business Report by the World Bank is the 17th annual edition that investigates regulations of relevance to enhance business activity, including investment in real estate, and those that constrain it. It also presents quantitative indicators on business regulations and the protection of real estate rights that can be compared across 189 economies, including 51 in Africa.

Selected real estate markets in the sub-Saharan region have shown improvements in investment opportunities in recent years. Countries from this region have taken the centre stage by improving transparency to push into the higher frontiers of real estate investment. Five out of eight sub-Sahara African markets – Kenya, Ghana, Nigeria, Zambia and Mauritius – ranked in the global top ten improvers by GRETI in 2014. This first-rate performance suggests that these countries are now targets for international corporate businesses in real estate investment.

Kenya emerged as the world's top transparency improver. Specific interventions that accounted for this sterling performance included increased availability of real estate market data. Potential real estate investors can systematically access rental data in Kenya – a significant attraction for international real estate investors. Credible data accessibility and consistency has been the driving force in the Kenyan real estate market in recent years. Another reason for its top global improver rating was the introduction of a framework for Real Estate Investment Trusts in 2013. At the same time, efforts were made to increasingly expand the country's land registry. The commitment to digitise all land records and establish a database on land rents was key in Kenya's outstanding performance.

In comparison, Ghana chalked an improved overall transparency index at the 7th position, accounted for primarily by the enhanced land registration coverage nationwide. Operationalised land registries had since 2013 been established in all ten regional capitals by the Lands Commission with the view to decentralising land administration services in the country. Another performance indicator was the effort to put in place a new urban planning framework to stimulate real estate investment. Further, the establishment of the Credit Reference Bureau, a database on borrowers in the country, earned the enviable third position on the top ten global transparency improvers. Ghana was accordingly credited as one of the countries in Africa that has good turnaround time in land registration, enforcing contracts and providing access to credit. These are critical ingredients for real estate market development.

Nigeria per GRETI rating is the 8th in sub-Saharan Africa and is reported to have made concerted efforts to improve real estate market transparency, with Lagos State as archetypal. In 2013, a new, comprehensive second Lagos State Development Plan (LSDP) was adopted to streamline the regulatory environment and also promote incentives for private sector participation in real estate investment and other businesses. Key drivers were land registration initiatives, creation of Geographical Information Systems (GIS) and the implementation of an e-approval system for development permits, though on a pilot basis.

Evidence provided by GRETI strongly suggests that South Africa remains the most transparent real estate market in sub-Saharan Africa. South Africa is ranked first and rated as the most transparent real estate market in Africa. It is further rated among the world's top 20 transparent markets and has consolidated its position with new legislation to establish the world's eighth largest REIT market.

An indication of how most countries in the subregion are not covered by GRETI might be reflected in the perceptions of global real estate investors and can be estimated by cross-referencing with the wider country coverage of the World Economic Forum's Global Competitiveness Index. Across countries where both are available, ranking for the two indices correlate strongly at 0.89. Two of African's top improvers globally – Kenya and Mauritius – outperformed emerging markets such as Argentina, Ukraine and Mongolia; the only exception is Ukraine, which ranked 76th under GCI, with Kenya and Mauritius at the 90th and 39th positions, respectively.

Most sub-Saharan African real estate markets are currently well within the investment horizons of mainstream global real estate investors, with more attraction for South Africa, Mauritius, Algeria, Morocco and Zambia. The Global Property Guide characterises real estate markets in Africa as generally having diverse investment potentials.

The increasing high attraction of overseas real estate investors to sub-Saharan Africa provides a stimulus for other countries apart from South Africa to demonstrate competing opportunities. Table 6.3 provides a summary that enables comparison of performance of real estate markets in selected African countries.

Rental yields, low transaction costs, low rental tax rate and pro-landlord market characteristics are the key investment drivers in the selected sub-Saharan African economies. Other drivers such as political risk, high transaction costs, high inflation and complex land title registration emerge as restraining forces for the real estate markets (see Table 6.3 for country specifics). Strong real estate investment demand is driven by substantial yield that is either high or moderate in South Africa, Ghana, Uganda, Kenya and Namibia.

All six real estate markets studied are pro-landlord. For instance, in Ghana and Nigeria, there are no effective rent controls. Lagos, however, had a 'Rent Control of Residential Premises Law,' which is currently not being implemented. Landlords and tenants in both countries freely agree on rent payable based on the willing landlord and willing tenant principle. Rents are often paid in advance, with landlords accepting advance payments for three months to two years. Dollar-indexed rents are typically paid in convertible local currencies for some investible properties in Ghana and Nigeria.

Table 6.3 Evidence of markets dynamics in six selected sub-Saharan African countries

	Country	*Market driving forces*	*Market restraining forces*
1	South Africa	i. High yields for luxury houses ii. Pro-landlord rental market iii. Moderate transaction costs iv. Strong rental market	Moderate to high income tax (7.23%)
2	Uganda	i. High yields in Kampala ii. Pro-landlord rental market	i. Limits on alien land ownership ii. Conflicts in Northern Region
3	Ghana	i. Pro-landlord rental market ii. High yields for Upmarket iii. Residential market dominated iv. Dollar indexed	i. Tenure issues ii. Inflation is higher than yields iii. Sporadic land titling system
4	Nigeria	i. Pro-landlord market ii. Moderate transaction costs iii. Strong rental market	i. Very high transaction costs ii. Low yields in Lagos iii. Issues with security and electricity supply
5	Kenya	i. Pro-landlord rental market ii. Moderate yields in Nairobi	i. Security and political concerns ii. High rental income tax (30%)
6	Namibia	i. High yields in Windhoek ii. Moderate transaction cost iii. Pro-landlord rental market	i. Interracial tension exists ii. Political and security issues

The pro-landlord rental markets in sub-Saharan African economies could be explained by market fundamentals. Rental income is certainly market-determined. The supply curve for real estate is highly inelastic and vertical in the short term, though it may flatten out over time. Demand for real estate is dependent on income, inflation, demographics and the local currency-US dollar exchange rate. Any factor that shifts the demand curve in the short term can impact rent or price rather than quantities.

In examining transaction costs and levels of rental income taxes as drivers for real estate markets development in selected countries, reliance was placed on the findings in the 2020 Doing Business Report. Transaction cost is measured as a percentage of the property value, with levels increasing from the least of 0.1 percent in Rwanda to 11.3 percent for Nigeria; others are Ghana (6.1 percent), South Africa (8.0 percent), Kenya (4.3 percent), Uganda (3.9 percent) and Namibia (5.8 percent). Transaction cost is an element of the overall investment capital outlay. Real estate markets in sub-Saharan Africa appear to charge relatively high tax rates; for instance, in Namibia, total tax payable in the real estate market as of 2015 was 20.7 percent of profit, the least, whilst South Africa levied 28.8 percent. Tax rates for other countries for the same period were in excess of 30 percent; for example, Ghana (33.3 percent), Nigeria (32.7 percent), Kenya (38.1 percent) and Uganda (36.5 percent).

Within an international context, the residential market in Ghana has achieved a return denominated in US dollars of 14.6 percent per annum from 1992 to 2007. From the viewpoint of a US-based investor, this may be compared with returns on US real estate over the same period of 11.2 percent per annum, and on US residential real estate of 12.2 percent per annum (NCREIF, 2008). In local currencies, the unweighted average annualised return on residential real estate in the five countries for which it is possible to measure total returns over the same period (Canada, France, Sweden, UK and US) was 11.9 percent per annum (IPD, 2008b; NCREIF, 2008). Thus, Ghanaian residential real estate investment in US$ denomination provided a return substantially above that on US residential investment. Indeed, above that of the local currency returns in all countries where data existed, apart from UK, where over the same period residential investment return was 16.9 percent.

Measured by standard deviation, the risk of US$-denominated Ghanaian residential investment had been 11.6 percent per annum, against only 3.0 percent per annum for US residential real estate as recorded by NCREIF. The volatility of the NCREIF US residential index was likely to be understated due to valuation smoothing. Geltner (1993) estimates a corrected standard deviation for the NCREIF returns at up to two times that shown by the Index. Similarly, the standard deviation averaged across the five countries where data existed was low, at 4.2 percent per annum. US-based investors in the Ghanaian residential market could have therefore received a return premium over the alternative of residential investment in US of the order of 2.4 percent per annum. Additionally with a risk penalty in added standard deviation from 8.6 percentage points per annum to 5.6 percentage points per annum, depending on the extent of desmoothing of the data thought to be appropriate in US.

On a risk-adjusted basis, US-based investors in Ghanaian residential real estate experienced a Sharpe Ratio (over US Treasury Bills) of 0.33. This compared with a Sharpe Ratio of 1.04 for US residential investments with no upward adjustment of volatility for smoothing, and 0.52 for US residential investments with an estimate of volatility doubled to correct for smoothing. The choice of Ghanaian residential investments over US alternative therefore, appeared to provide US-domiciled investors a slightly inferior risk-adjusted return, although the size of the margin between the two was uncertain given problems in estimating true volatility for US results. Since the Sharpe Ratio on US long-dated government bonds over the same period had been 0.39, and that on US equities estimated at 0.38, however, both US and Ghanaian real estate investments had offered risk-adjusted returns comfortably above those on the other major asset classes.

As the superior real estate risk adjusted returns in US suggested, the period from 1992 to 1997 covered by the Ghanaian residential index was characterised by strong real estate performance. Also, since 2001, relatively weak returns on equity investments had occurred in the wake of the global stock market declines in the early 2000s. Indeed, exceptionally high rates of appreciation in real estate prices across many countries from the mid-1990s up to the mid-2000s were seen as 'the biggest financial bubble in history' (The Economist, 2005); a diagnosis that relied primarily on simple indicators such as deviations in prices from long-run trends and high real estate prices to household income ratios.

The establishment of a credible database; research funding from institutional investors to support quantitative research; government's commitment to make real estate markets play a relevant role in national development; strong partnerships between academia and industry; and the application of financial models in real estate market analysis will positively impact real estate market development in sub-Saharan Africa.

Note

1 $RE_i = GDP_i \times 0.45$ [1]

for developed countries; and

$RE_i = GDP_i \times 0.45\ (GDH_i / 20{,}000)^{1/3}$ [2]

for developing countries

where:
RE_i = country investible commercial real estate value;
GDP_i = country Gross Domestic Product; and
GDH_i = country Gross Domestic Product per capita.

'Developed' countries are defined as those with GDP per capita above US$ 20,000 and 'developing' countries below this threshold.

References

Anim-Odame, W. (2009). *Residential real estate investment in emerging economies: The case of Ghana*. Unpublished PhD Thesis, Cass Business School, Faculty of Finance, City University, London.

Crosby, N. and Keogh, G. (1990). *The relationship between shop values and rates: Final report*, unpublished report to ESRC/RICS. Reading, UK: University of Reading.

Databank Group. (2004). *African stock markets consolidate gains*. Accra: Databank Group.

Databank Group. (2008). *Annual review of the economy and stock market in Ghana*. Accra: Databank Group.

The Economist. (2005). After the fall. *The Economist*, June 16.

Gardiner, C. and Henneberry, J. (1988). The development of a simple regional office rent prediction model. *Journal of Valuation*, 7 (1), pp. 36–52.

Gardiner, C. and Henneberry, J. (1991). Predicting regional office rents using habit-persistence theory. *Journal of Property Valuation and Investment*, 9 (3), pp. 215–226.

Geltner, D. (1993). Estimating market values from appraised values without assuming an efficient market. *Journal of Real Estate Research*, 8 (3), pp. 325–345.

Ghana Stock Exchange. (2006). *Information bulletin*. Accra: Ghana Stock Exchange.

Global Property Guide. (2015). *Property markets in sub-Saharan Africa*. Makati, Philippines: Global Property Guide.

Hetherington, J. T. (1988). Forecasting of rents. In: A. MacLeary and N. Nanthakumaran ed., *Property investment theory*. London: Spon.

Hughes, F. and Arissen, J. (2005). *Global real estate securities – Where do they fit in the broader market?* Brussels: European Public Real Estate Association.

IPD. (2008a). *Index guide*. London: Investment Property Databank Limited.

IPD. (2008b). *Global property index*. London: Investment Property Databank Limited.

Jones Lang LaSalle. (2014). *Global real estate transparency index*.

Jones Lang LaSalle. (2018). *Global real estate transparency index. Global Research*.

Liang, Y. and Gordon, N. (2003). *A bird's eye of global real estate markets*. Parsippany, NJ: Prudential Real Estate Investors.

NCREIF. (2008). *NPI returns, national council of real estate investment fiduciaries from*. www.ncreif.com accessed December 12, 2008.

Stock Exchange Act, 1971 (Act 384), Ghana.

Transparency International. (2020). *Corruption perceptions index*. Berlin: Transparency International.

World Economic Forum. (2015). *Global competitiveness index*. Cologne: World Economic Forum.

Yartey, C. A. (2006). *The stock market and the financing of corporate growth in Africa: The case of Ghana*. Washington, DC: International Monetary Fund (WP/06/201), Working Paper.

7 Valuation and compensation

7.1 Introduction

Real estate issues that form the bedrock in promoting valuation in Ghana are the cornerstone of this chapter. The quality of structures that support valuation activities in an economy determines the real estate market's maturity and its role in national development. This chapter offers insightful and factual information on property valuation in the country and the basis for peer review in the sub-Saharan African countries. In turn, it is an opportunity to fix the gaps in promoting real estate valuation in the subregion. Specific strategic interventions that have been implemented in Ghana to support real estate valuation are covered for the benefit of industry practitioners, investors, academia and other market players.

Property valuation is the art of determining property value. It is conducted for businesses, individuals, financial institutions and governments for several purposes. In the US, the term appraisal is used. The debate on whether valuation is a true art or science remains inconclusive. More sophisticated methods of valuation are being used these days to make valuation be deemed as more of a science. But long experience definitely results in a Valuer developing a 'feel' to know instinctively that he has arrived at the right valuation opinion, making the process be seen as an art. The value of a property to be determined is expected to be the proxy for its price. This process is essentially premised on demand and supply factors, thus, determined on market value basis.

Certain terminologies in the real estate market are often misunderstood, just because they are not as simple to comprehend as they appear. There is a distinction between the value, price and worth of a property. The value is an estimated amount that is the most probable price to be reasonably obtained. Value is therefore an estimate of transaction price. It excludes forced sales and special situations. Property value is a professional opinion that is estimated based on market evidence, either valuation-based or transaction-based. Its determination requires rigorous analysis and assumes both parties in the transaction are reasonably informed about the nature of the property, its actual and potential uses as well as the state of the market.

A property transaction has to take place to establish its price. Accordingly, the price of a property is always a spot figure. In other words, price is an observed transaction price. Sellers set maximum bid prices based on their assessment of the worth of the property to them. Buyers, on the other hand, set minimum sale prices based on their assessment of worth. The parties make these assumptions because the buyer and seller have different forecasts or positions regarding the worth of the subject property. This market behaviour assumes a normal distribution of real estate prices. Transactions are habitually concluded at a price that is pegged between the sellers' maximum price and buyers' minimum price.

The worth of a property, on the other hand, is sometimes referred to as the investment value. It is the bid price of an individual investor for a property, and is therefore investor- specific. In practice, the worth of a property is estimated by employing the Discounted Cash Flow (DCF) approach. It reflects the consensus view on future changes in property cash flow due to rental growth and occupancy. An appropriate discount rate based on general risk-free rates is frequently employed, plus a premium for the risk, illiquidity and costs of the investment in the estimation of worth. Investors normally postulate different forecasts of the market and/or property. The worth to an individual investor reflects specific assumptions including the expectations for the future growth in income or changes in the yield; judgements of the risk of the investment; and views on ability to increase value through active property management.

The credibility, reliability and accuracy of property values are imperative and more germane, particularly in emerging economies. The state of market equilibrium assumes a perfect competition and a balance of supply and demand. Conditions for this assumption include homogeneity of products and an unlimited number of vendors and vendees. In contrast, such conditions tend to be inapplicable in the real estate market. It is so for a number of reasons. First, there is always an imbalance in the supply and demand for property, regardless of its use – residential, commercial, industrial or recreational. Thus, it takes a reasonable time to increase property supply in the market. Acquisition of planning and development permits, availability and cost of financing as well as construction periods are some of the causes. Second, a physical real estate marketplace does not exist in any country. Other investment vehicles such as equities, stocks or shares and other fixed instruments, for example, treasury bills or bonds, are all traded at a designated physical marketplace such as the Cental Bank, Stock Exchange Market and Financial Market. Third, real estate is fixed in location and size, giving it a heterogeneous state. In fact, no two or more properties are indistinguishable. Each property, in all terms, is unique, and not exactly the same as another. The gross floor area, orientation, legal or equitable interest, aesthetics such as landscaping, fittings and fixtures, as well as amenities and finishes will not necessarily be the same. Fourth, a real estate asset may be held as an investment vehicle with the primary objective of realising income in the form of rent and also capital gains in terms of appreciation in value over time. For owner-occupiers, a property would be acquired for self-occupation and to achieve capital appreciation.

A deeper understanding of the distinction between real estate and other investment markets is equally relevant in property valuation. Time value of money as the basic concept of property valuation requires adequate data. The Valuer or Appraiser is required to assemble and analyse credible and reliable data in arriving at the valuation opinion. Data accessibility, credibility and reliability are therefore the three cardinal factors in property valuation. Emerging economies such as Ghana are challenged with limited property data accessibility in relation to mature markets such as UK, US and others. This market situation tends to suggest that property-related procedures such as conveyancing, tenancy agreement, rent determination, valuation and compliance with stamp duty provisions are generally weak or difficult to implement. The practice of valuation can be made effective and achieve true proxies for prices only when Valuers are guaranteed access to comprehensive, reliable and timely evidence of comparables.

Lack of comparable evidence is a limitation because only a few transactions occur in the formal market, with predominance of the informal market. Sometimes, lack of transparency due to unrecorded transactions may characterise the market. Nonetheless, lack of comparables should not avert the conduction of property valuation. The skills, expertise and judgement of the Valuer become especially important in an opaque or low transparent market, where comparables are either limited or virtually unavailable.

In Ghana, the Valuer is also known as the Valuation and Estate Surveyor. As a key professional in the real estate market with specialised training and skills, the Valuation and Estate Surveyor is also in the best position for the role of a property manager. Valuers are expected to be conversant with estates and interests; the content of leases and statutory planning, and development controls; as well as landlord and tenant legislation, with the care of duty to consult with other professionals when necessary. The management functions also include advising on provision of utility services, contractual arrangements, rental values determination at revisions and on expiration and property preservation to achieve the highest and best use.

The validity of a valuation opinion is dependent on how well it can be supported by market data. The Valuers' experience, which includes their stored market knowledge of historical and current transactions, is equally relevant, whilst chronological evidence of market transactions is also an asset. Legislative restrictions or technology limitations may set barriers to the release of property data into the public domain. In Ghana, the Stamp Duty (Amendment) Act, 2008 (Act 764), does not compel parties to disclose all relevant details such as type, situation, size and nature of the subject properties. This situation offers a difficulty for Valuers to obtain comprehensive information in order to fully analyse stated consideration without physically inspecting the property. Reliance on personal knowledge of neighbourhoods in the city and experience in most cases do not provide the leeway. Every real estate valuation report is to be certified by a qualified Valuer who is duly registered with a statutory institution and also in good standing. In Ghana, the statutory regulator of Valuers is the Ghana Institution of Surveyors (GhIS). Valuers with overseas professional qualifications are mandated to register with GhIS for certification to practice in Ghana.

In the United Kingdom, the Royal Institution of Surveyors (RICS) has since 1974 published its valuation standards, colloquially known as the 'Red Book.' Market value is defined in the Red Book as 'the estimated amount for which a property should exchange on the date of valuation between a willing buyer and a willing seller in an arm's-length transaction after proper marketing wherein the parties had each acted knowledgeably, prudently and without compulsion' (Royal Institution of Chartered Surveyors, 2018). A school of thought in recent years has argued against market value as the appropriate basis of real estate valuation, but rather held a strong view in favour of Discounted Cash Flow (DCF) analysis. This position gives more credence to the estimation of market worth. Mackmin and Emary (2000), for example, argues in favour of DCF and asserts that

> where the parties had each acted knowledgeably and prudently, it presumes that both the willing buyer and the willing seller are reasonably informed about the nature and characteristics of the asset, its actual and potential uses, and the state of the market as of the date of the valuation. Each is further presumed to act for self-interest with that knowledge, and prudently to seek the best price for their respective positions in the transaction. Prudence is assessed by referring to the state of the market at the date of the valuation, not with benefit of hindsight at some later date. It is not necessarily imprudent for a seller to sell property in a market with falling prices at a price that is lower than previous market levels. In such cases, as is true for other purchase and sale situations in markets with changing prices, the prudent buyer or seller will act in accordance with the best information available at the time.

Critics hold the view that by this definition of market value, it is assumed that buyers and sellers would use all the available information at the time of the transaction. But in practice, it may prove to be otherwise, where other property owners and potential buyers had advisors with other information or rather placed a different interpretation on the information available. That information may not, at the date of valuation, be part of the market data. Again, market value is an opinion, and it is not uncommon that different Valuers in the same real estate market may arrive at different opinions. However, the divergence in value ought not to be wide, because the underlying principles of the traditional methods of valuation remain globally the same. The process of value determination obliges the Valuer to inspect the subject property, make any enquiries arising out of that inspection and conduct a market survey to gather as much relevant information as possible, including recent transactions, to present an opinion on the market value.

7.2 Traditional methods of valuation

The appropriate method of valuation to be adopted in arriving at the value of a property is dependent on the purpose of valuation. Purposes for which a property can be valued include letting, taxation, sale, purchase, loan security (mortgage), accounting, compensation, rating and insurance. Rental valuation may be needed where a property is to be let on a lease or tenancy arrangement. It means an advice will be required to be given to either the tenant or landlord or both on the rent payable. Standard clauses are usually provided in leases or tenancy agreements that require rents to be revised and to inform parties. An advice on the new rent payable is therefore inevitable. Rental valuation in addition provides the basis for the determination of rental income tax payable by landlords to the tax authorities. In Ghana, 8 percent of gross rent is payable as rental income tax to the Ghana Revenue Authority for residential properties and 15 percent for offices, retail and industrial uses that are generally termed commercial purposes.

In contrast to rental valuation, capital valuation is undertaken for the other valuation purposes. Capital valuation is a prerequisite to determine the basis of property- related taxes such as stamp duty (payable by transferee), gift tax (payable by donee), capital gains tax (payable by transferor) and property rate (payable by property owner). Whilst property rate is paid annually, the others are one-off payments when a transaction is executed. Capital valuation is also relevant in property sale transactions where both the vendor and purchaser require a professional advice on the value; a proxy for the price to be realised. Whilst the target of vendors is to realise the maximum price (ceiling price) for the property, that of potential purchasers (vendees) is whether the asking price is reasonable or whether trying to negotiate a lower price level (floor price) is likely to be fruitful.

Real estate is a good security for a loan. People buy houses by borrowing money or a large percentage of it through a mortgage from a bank or non-bankimg financial institution. The bank or nonbanking financial institution as the lender or mortgagee will need to assess the risk involved on the basis that if the borrower or mortgagor defaults on repayment, the property can be sold to realise enough money to cover the outstanding debt.

Valuation for accounting purposes is relevant as companies are statutorily mandated to publish their accounts annually. The value of assets of companies are determined by Valuers and incorporated in the annual accounts. Most companies are unable to contract Valuers to undertake capital valuation on assets each year but rather permit accountants to apply depreciation to arrive at the current value of the assets. On this trajectory, the companies are nonetheless constrained to value all assets at least every five years to realise current capital values.

Article 20 (2) of the 1992 Constitution of the Republic of Ghana stipulates that compulsory acquisition of property by the state shall only be made under a law which makes provision for the prompt payment of fair and adequate compensation. An expropriated property owner whose interest was compulsorily acquired is statutory required to submit a valid claim (see section 7.7). A capital valuation is required to provide the basis and quantum of the claim for compensation to make it valid.

A prudent decision can be made by insuring your real estate asset. Capital valuation is essential to provide the basis for the premium for insurance purposes. Real estate is generally considered as a long-term asset for its sustainability. Insurance companies demand it is insured at the value that covers its cost of replacement. This will normally consist of the cost of demolishing the damaged building and rebuilding it, including all fees and an allowance for inflation. An insurance valuation is therefore quite different from a valuation for other purposes in that it is based on construction costs and not market value.

Whereas there is only one method for rental valuations (comparative method), there are five traditional methods of determining the capital value of a property; these are discussed next.

Comparative method

The comparative method of valuation is underpinned by the principle of comparing an apple to an apple. Thus, it is based on the basic principle of comparing similar properties in value-determination and reckoned as the most appropriate methodology if credible data is readily available. Rental valuations are conducted by employing the comparative or comparison method, except in very unusual circumstances. If a warehouse, for example, is recently let at US$ 850,000 per annum, then a similar warehouse in the same or similar neighbourhood would be expected to be let on the same terms, including the annual rent of US$ 850,000. However, no two real estate assets are deemed to be identical in all respects. Therefore, an adjustment will have to be made for the differences. Usually, factors such as age, construction details, orientation of accommodation, utilities, services and very importantly location and accessibility would determine the rental value. For that reason, Valuers are expected to adjust their figures to take account of those differences in arriving at an opinion on the rental value.

This method is also one of the five basic methods of capital valuation. In capital valuation, the comparative method is generally used for non-income-producing properties and for large transaction volumes of very similar properties. For owner-occupied properties and vacant land, it stands as the best method for capital value determination. A unit of comparison is often applied and this is adjusted as necessary to reflect differences in properties. Units of comparison include hectares or acres for land; square metres or square feet for residential, office and industrial (including warehouse) properties; foot frontage for retail properties, including shops and malls; number of beds for hotels; dining spaces for restaurants; and seats for theatres and cinemas. The use of the comparative method for hotels, restaurants, theatres and cinemas is becoming unpopular and giving way to the profits method, which is now common.

Profits method

This method is employed where the value of the property is driven by the profits of a specific occupier, often because the occupier is, to some extent, a monopoly. It is used only where there is no better approach, as it relates the value of the property to the profit of a business using the premises. The method estimates a rental value appropriate to the property, which can be converted to a capital value.

The profits method is suitable for properties generally known as a going concern business, including public houses, cinemas, hotels, restaurants, harbours, zoos, amusement parks, petrol stations, gas stations and racecourses. These businesses possess a monopoly element that will have a strong impact on their trading. The monopoly can be attributed to the use to which the premises is put, its location, design of building or a combination of these characteristics. The trading potentials of these properties can make them attractive to purchasers and are thus valued using the profits method.

Profits method of property valuation is undertaken with recourse to the latest audited accounts of the business first, by estimating the gross receipts of the business; and second deducting from these the working expenses, including a figure for repairs and renewals to any equipment used in the business and to the property. The result provides a net profit from which is deducted an amount that a tenant would require for himself, technically known as the tenant's share, which may range from 10 percent to as much as 60 percent; the residue is the amount which is available for rent. This rent is capitalised to determine the market value. The tenant's share covers three main items: first, pure interest on the capital invested to allow the tenant a risk-free security; second, risk over and above the pure interest to reward the tenant for the additional risk involved in the particular type of business; and third, the tenant's own reward for running the business because they must be allowed a proper remuneration for their efforts in running the business.

From the latest audited accounts, delete therefrom any items that do not relate to the running of the business; for example, over the years a company may have invested part of its profits and interest from such investments, which will appear as a receipt in the accounts. This amount should be deducted from the accounts because the rental to be estimated relates to the property and not to the accumulated investments of a particular occupier. Any expenses that do not relate to the business as such would also have to be taken out of the accounts and any rent actually paid must also be excluded. Rent is what is to be determined by the calculation and should not therefore be deducted as a working expense. The residue as rent is capitalised in line with the investment method (see the next section) at the appropriate yield to arrive at the market value of the business.

There is no substitute for audited accounts as an input for the estimation of net profit. That part of tenants' share that relates to pure interest is unlikely to change from one type of property to another, but that part which relates to their risk may well vary.

Investment or income capitalisation method

This method is often used to value income-producing properties and is considered to be the most widely employed after the comparative method. It considers an income-producing property as an investment with its value depending on the expected returns. The purpose of an investment valuation is to provide an opinion on the capital value of the right to receive annual streams of income. Where evidence on income and yield is available, the capital value of the property can be determined using the investment method. Therefore, if two of the three variables – capital, income and yield – are known, the third can easily be determined.

With real estate, the capital and net rent are closely related by the yield. In the process of market value estimation, net rent is either known or can be estimated by the comparison method. Yield is, in fact, dependent on the security and regularity of the stream of income and for the real estate market in Ghana, it ranges between 5 percent and 12 percent. For residential, yields are between 5 percent and 9 percent, depending on the location and quality of property. Yields for offices range from 8 percent to 10 percent and depend on location, facilities, tenants and size. Slightly higher yields of between 9 percent and 12 percent are reported for the retail submarket, and dependent on location and tenant. Similar yields of between 10 percent and 12 percent prevail for the industrial market, depending on location, design, size and age. These yields present an indication of the range and pattern between various real estate submarkets in the country. Yields in general are affected by several factors including location, quality of property, tenant, facilities, size, age and design, and may be subject to changes over time.

Cost or contractor's method

This method estimates the replacement costs of the property and adds to it the value of the land. It is employed for properties with no observed transactions and as such no market evidence of value, for example, specialised buildings including cathedrals, schools, hospitals, airports, power stations, mosques, lighthouses and palaces. These are properties that rarely change hands. The method assumes that value relates to cost, though value depends on supply and demand.

This has been the conventional method in less mature or nascent real estate markets such as Ghana. The valuation process involves assessing the cost of replacing the property and adjustment for the age and obsolescence – economic, functional and physical – added to the market value of the land in its highest and best use. Although the cost method determines a capital value, this can be converted to a rent by estimating the annual equivalent of the market value. Though the method is most appropriate for rating valuation in the country, it is meant to be reluctantly employed as the only method in real estate value determination. This is so because it is generally referred to as the method of last resort in general valuation. Hence, the cost or contractor's method can be used only when the other four traditional methods are inapplicable.

Residual method

This method is employed for properties with development potential, usually vacant land or properties that can be redeveloped, refurbished or extended. The property may be let at a rent that is unlikely to be a guide for its valuation or it may be equally unlikely that a similar property has been recently transacted to provide an indication of what the property is valued at. For this reason, the Valuer may have to mimic the market; the possibilities of developing or redeveloping the site is to be explored. The approach generally estimates a capital value but this can readily be converted to a rental value, if necessary.

The residual method is premised on the theory that the value of the existing property is represented by the value of the completed development less the cost of the development, developer's profit and all fees and interest on money borrowed. The residue is the amount available for the purchase of the undeveloped interest. Critics of the method argue that the method can be too simplistic in its approach to timing of costs, including finance charges. The use of discounted cash flow techniques, however, addresses this shortcoming.

7.3 Valuation guidelines and standards

Real estate market maturity is dependent on the strength and structure of the economy, foreign investment levels and controls, market size, and the quality of infrastructure. For instance, in Southeast Asian countries, the market evolution has been a function of city growth or urbanisation, emergence of the investment market and shifts in principal areas of national economic activity. In this context, Valuers are expected to undertake their professional work with due skills, care, diligence and expedition with recourse to technical and professional standards. Fit-for-purpose real estate valuation guidelines and standards are a necessity within and across subregions of similar market characteristics.

With an initial focus on valuations incorporated in published accounts, the Red Book has since the mid-1990s been applied to virtually all valuations and subsequently since 1991 become mandatory. The guiding principles of high standards of integrity, clarity and objectivity define the purpose of the Red

Book. It defines the criteria to establish membership qualification, bases of valuations, assumptions and other considerations in value determination, minimum reporting standards, and criteria for disclosure for third parties. It further sets out the procedural rules and guidance for compliance by RICS members. Nonetheless, the Red Book, which broadly defines a framework for best practices in valuation, fails to instruct members on the methodology or technique to apply on a case-by-case basis.

The experience in Ghana has followed a different trajectory. The Guidance notes on valuation practices in Ghana were developed in 1995 for members of the Ghana Institution of Surveyors (GhIS). Members are regulated differently within the framework of the professional code of ethics and the rules of conduct. Whilst recognising the limitations and gaps in valuation practices in the country, the Land Valuation Division (LVD) of the Lands Commission in the second half of 2010 took steps to develop and implement its valuation guidelines and standards; a novelty in the public sector land administration. As of 2010, the GhIS Guidance notes on valuation had been in operation for a decade and a half without any revision to reflect emerging global and local issues on property valuation. Provisions of the new valuation guidelines and standards of the Lands Commission were carefully crafted in line with the contents of the current edition of the Red Book but with ingredients that focused on local market dynamics.

Valuation professionals within LVD were engaged in a series of technical workshops to provide inputs towards the development of the first-ever valuation guidelines and standards. The director of the division, as the lead Valuer, working with a carefully selected team, demonstrated an exemplary leadership drive, commitment and professionalism. Such leadership qualities were an important ingredient for a successful process that was consultative and consensus-building from inception to the end.

As the most current blueprint for property valuation services delivery in Ghana, the document was intended to guide Valuers in the public sector to deliver high-quality valuation of landed properties, plants and machinery. The Lands Commission valuation guidelines and standards are widely used by a cross section of Valuers, including those in the private sector in the country. A number of technical workshops were organised as part of the process to consider specialised papers on property inspection, referencing and data collection, data collation and analysis, valuation methodology, valuation reporting and certification. Brainstorming sessions followed as activities under stage one.

Thematic areas were identified at stage one to form the basis of the framework under stage two. In the design of the framework, further consultations were undertaken among Valuers within the Lands Commission to redefine and deepen the contents of the framework. At this stage, references were made to the Red Book, Guidance notes on valuation practice in Ghana by GhIS and International Valuation Standards for best practices.

Stage three was devoted to consultations with industry practitioners and academia to seek opinions and additional inputs with the view to enriching the contents. Expert inputs from the mining and agricultural sectors were also solicited within the gamut of valuation for compensation purposes in those sectors. In collating views and opinions from the industry and academia, references were also made to the statutes on land administration regarding interest holding, valuation, compulsory acquisition and compensation determination.

The next stage provided a platform to reconsider views and opinions based on the agreed-upon framework. A retreat was organised under stage four to further brainstorm on inputs collated and for the drafting of the valuation guidelines and standards. At this stage, key lawyers within the Lands Commission were co-opted into the team to review and assist in drafting the document; a great synergy between the Valuers and lawyers was achieved.

A wider consultation with public and private sector Valuers was conducted as the penultimate stage to review and adopt the draft document for finalisation. The principal expected outcome of this stage was to ensure that all valuation technical issues had adequately been addressed. In addition, the consultation sought to achieve ownership of the document by all staff of the Lands Commission for smooth implementation.

The final stage was devoted to seeking approval from the governing board of the Commission. In seeking approval, the document was split into four sections for the sake of presentation to the 17-member board, with the leadership of the Commission and drafting team as resource persons. The representatives of the Ghana Institution of Surveyors and Ghana Bar Association on the board, as past presidents of their respective bodies, played a significant role. The entire process commenced in September 2010; approval from the board was obtained in December 2011, and implementation in January 2012.

As the Red Book has evolved from 1974 to date and stood the test of time, the valuation guidelines and standards of the Lands Commission have been crafted to allow for changes over time to account for emerging issues and challenges. The contemporary edition has accordingly provided a solid foundation to make future revisions less tedious to undertake. Resource availability and visionary leadership are the paramount drivers needed to sustain the process. This achievement should ultimately lead to building a strong partnership with the Ghana Institution of Surveyors to develop and launch comprehensive, up-to-date valuation guidelines and standards for the country.

Teamwork is very important in the process of developing a similar document, for the first time, in an emerging economy. Team members are to be carefully selected with a blend of diverse qualifications, experience, expertise and skills. It is important to set unambiguous objectives from inception to provide an opportunity to answer most, if not all, of the frequently asked questions on property value determination. A document of this nature is to be characterised by a set of valuation best practices that guarantees quality valuation services. Interestingly, the launch of the Lands Commission valuation guidelines and standards in January 2012 yielded a final closure to the use of *Open Market*

Value as the basis of valuation in Ghana, even when RICS had long before replaced that with *Market Value*.

7.4 Electronic real estate database

A credible and accessible database is essential for real estate valuation in all economies. Records of property transactions on sales and rentals provide both financial and descriptive information that are generally needed to accomplish valuation assignments. Access to a well-established system of real estate database by Valuers will provide comparables and other relevant information for property valuation. Such a system must at all times not only be subjected to strict quality control but also be characterised by clear, standardised definitions to ensure consistency and comparability within and across real estate markets.

In Ghana, Valuers of the Lands Commission are required to extract credible or verifiable data from transactions submitted for stamp duty as inputs into the electronic real estate database that was established in 2011. Additionally, comparable data that are obtained from other credible sources – public or private institutions or individuals – are to be verified and input into the database. In-house assessed property values are initially reviewed by a team of officers at Valuers Review Meetings, and subsequently considered by the Valuation Technical Committee of the Lands Commission. Such approved values are also relevant and should be downloaded into the electronic database.

The electronic database features three broad property data classifications, namely property description, size, and sale and rent data. Each classification reveals specific features for emphasis. Advantages for establishing an electronic real estate database are numerous. Primarily, it promotes property performance analysis, and provides the framework for the generation of property benchmarks and market indices and the needed ingredients for the production of real estate market reports. These reports are commonly needed not only by academia for teaching and learning, but also by the industry in making prudent investment decisions. The guiding principle of establishing an electronic database is to provide information with clarity. Commenting on property investment markets in transitional East European economies, Adair *et al.* (2004) asserts strongly that data transparency is a key characteristic of a mature market, and markets that are able to demonstrate that they possess such data have a competitive advantage and are more likely to attract private sector investment funds.

The establishment of a digital real estate database is a catalyst for timely and accurate delivery of valuation services. It moreover offers easy access to credible data on property values as the basis for the determination of premiums in the execution of leases or lease renewals. In particular, it benefits stamp duty assessment by making the process easier and more transparent to maximise revenue generation for the central government.

Real estate market maturity is of great concern to investors, developers, market intermediaries, academia and governments in emerging economies, particularly in sub-Saharan Africa. Anim-Odame (2009), in modelling residential transaction-based data from the paper-based archival records at the Land Valuation Division of the Lands Commission, prescribed a framework for the establishment of an electronic real estate database in Ghana. The framework provides a platform for digital capturing of valuation-based data, that includes property description, size, location and neighbourhood characteristics as the mandatory inputs. Property characteristics for comparison include location, size, transaction date, type, age, condition, building specification, layout and interest. The electronic real estate database also allows for photographs taken on the site during inspection to be downloaded to aid as pictorial views.

7.5 Computer-assisted valuation system

The evolution of information technology has offered an opportunity for economies to develop and establish an architectural framework for computer-assisted valuation systems. Valuation methodology and techniques are the underlining guiding principles in developing an appropriate product based on real estate market dynamics. A computer-assisted valuation system has been developed in Ghana and is being piloted for government infrastructural projects by the Land Valuation Division. It allows for searches of comparable data and analysis of rates per square metre and to generate valuation reports for mass appraisals, among others. As a pilot activity, its usage was initially limited to Accra, the regional and national capital of Ghana, for mass valuations concerning compulsory acquisition of land and properties. Its application has been relevant in the execution of several road projects and other infrastructural projects of national interest, including utility installations.

In particular, the system provides for the speedy and timely generation of valuation reports. By automating the processes, valuation reports for several properties on the basis of mass appraisal are less cumbersome and generated timely. The deployment of an automated real estate valuation system further promotes effective and efficient delivery of other land administration related services in addition to being a useful tool in realising the scope for cost savings in the process. The usefulness of computer-assisted valuation systems is strongly relevant in property rating for revenue mobilisation by the local government such as the Metropolitan, Municipal and District Assemblies in Ghana. Overall, the usefulness of the system could be extended to support superiors at the Land Valuation Division and allied land sector agencies to set performance targets for their subordinates and also be employed as a monitoring tool for the progress of services delivery.

7.6 Real estate research and development

Property is not homogeneous and therefore no two properties are exactly alike. Each property is unique because of its physical location and other attributes such as size, usage, shape, tenure and aesthetics. The location of a property plays an important role as value and rent determinant. The value of a property is thus heavily influenced, either favourably or unfavourably, by changes in the neighbourhood characteristics. Each real estate market is therefore local. It suffices to say that the real estate market, unlike other investment markets, is a collection of individual submarkets.

The nature of the real estate market has been one where information is expected to be less freely available than in other investment markets. It is revealing that most countries in sub-Saharan Africa lack active real estate investment markets and primary sources of market evidence. These are the two major factors that shape real estate research in advanced economies. Two of the firms of global intermediaries – Knight Frank and Investment Property Databank (IPD) – are widely and globally known to have produced market indicators for few sub-Saharan African countries, including South Africa. Though disappointing, it is not surprising that published research on African real estate investment markets is limited. Outside South Africa, published research on real estate investment markets in the subregion has mainly been concerned with institutional structures and constraints on market development (Anim-Odame, 2009).

Real estate valuation thrives on a solid foundation of property research and development, but in Ghana it does not seem to be so. There are limited research works on the real estate market, and valuation in particular. Even with a huge existing capacity, the potentials are yet to be tapped. Public institutions such as the Lands Commission and Ghana Revenue Authority are well-placed to take the necessary steps to establish and resource their research and development departments to promote real estate market research activities. Techniques in real estate valuation and market analysis as well as real estate revenue mobilisation are some of the thematic areas worth considering by these two important state institutions.

A similar trajectory is anticipated in the real estate valuation industry and academia where the Ghana Institution of Surveyors and the Department of Land Economy exist as key players. An agenda for rigorous real estate research and development should, for example, provide a vehicle to analyse market performance and its submarkets for the residential, commercial, retail and industrial uses, among others. Tracking and forecasting of prices, rental values, levels of supply and demand of property units, investment yields and vacancy rates are other research topics that are of great concern to real estate investors, developers and governments in most economies, particularly in sub-Saharan African countries including Ghana, where some of these indicators are only available in a limited scope.

7.7 Compulsory acquisition and compensation

Compulsory acquisition may be defined as the purchase or taking, under statutory powers, a piece of land or an interest in land without the agreement of the owner. The statutory powers are needed for reasons such as:

1 Authorising the compulsory acquisition.
2 Legalising an activity that would otherwise be unlawful and could be restrained by the courts.

3 Giving powers to authorities of statutory creation to undertake a particular activity.

One of the greatest land administration challenges confronting the Government of Ghana (GoG) in the use of its powers of compulsory acquisition to expropriate private interest in landed property is the ability to pay fair and adequate compensation promptly. The 1992 Constitution reinforces commensurate compensation payment based on the principle of equivalent reinstatement.

Compulsory acquisition of a landed asset by GoG through its Ministries, Departments and Agencies (MDAs) in the public interest is thus subject to the payment of fair, adequate and prompt compensation. This principle is well-known in the country. In general, apart from buildings, land and crops (food and cash), other structures of all types can be adversely affected by a compulsory acquisition to warrant compensation payment.

The State Lands Act, 1962 (Act 125) and the State Lands (Amendment) Act, 2000 (Act 586) are usually relied on in addition to the Constitution as the principal statutes for all acquisitions in the country. Statutory requirements in these laws are restricted to the acquisition of 'private' interest in landed properties. Contrarily, an 'acquisition' of a stool land is undertaken by using the Administration of Lands Act, 1962 (Act 123). Under Act 125 and Act 586, a lump sum compensation is paid to claimants. Section 10 of Act 123, on the contrary, prescribes the payment of annual compensation rental for stool land acquisition in line with the customary belief that stool land belongs to the community, of which many are dead, a few are living and countless hosts are still unborn.

Acquisition procedures

Though the stages involved in compulsory acquisition may seem to be simplified, they are extensive and could be cumbersome in some cases. The originating point in procedures for compulsory acquisition for public purposes is the MDA through the Regional Coordinating Council that sets in motion a Site Advisory Committee to identify, select and recommend an appropriate site. The Regional Lands Officer in the respective region serves as the Secretary to the Committee. Recommendations from the Committee are submitted to the Lands Commission for consideration and forwarded to the minister responsible for lands and natural resources, who approves the recommendations after being satisfied and causes an appropriate Executive Instrument of the acquisition to be published.

Compulsory acquisition procedures are envisioned to be transparent and therefore subjected to wide publicity to attract the attention of all affected persons. Since it is very important the government should not acquire lands stealthily or by default on the part of landowners, rules are promulgated to ensure adequate publicity of the acquisition. Under Section 2 of Act 125, the Executive Instrument is published and publicised in the following prescribed manner:

1 Be served personally on any person having an interest in the land; or
2 Be left with any person in occupation of the land; and

3 Be affixed at a convenient place on the land; and
4 Be published on three consecutive occasions in a newspaper circulating in the district where the land is situated.

Notice of the acquisition is therefore to be served personally on the expropriated owner or the other three steps – (2), (3) and (4) – above followed, but not only (1) or (2).

Three distinct features in the acquisition processes under Act 125 are to be clearly noted. First, who has the power to acquire the property in question? The Act explicitly provides the authority that is exclusively vested in the president of the Republic of Ghana as the only person who can exercise the power of compulsory acquisition. Owing to the complexities of the processes of expropriation, this power is exercisable for and on the president's behalf by the minister responsible for lands and natural resources. Second, by what procedure can acquisition be completed? The publication of the Executive Instrument brings a finality to the acquisition process by extinguishing the interest of the owner in the property, and thus prevents further alterations or creation of any new interest in the affected property so as to increase the burden of compensation payable by the state. Third, what are the provisions on compensation assessment? Assessment of the value of the acquired property for compensation purposes must always conform with the legal rules governing this matter (see Article 20 of the 1992 Constitution and provisions in Act 125 and Act 586). Beyond the acquisition, the valuation is expected to be carried out with reasonable technical competence.

Compensation assessment

The litmus test for prompt payment of fair and adequate compensation is captured under Article 20 (2) (a) of the Constitution. It provides that compulsory acquisition of property by the state shall only be made under a law which makes provision for the prompt payment of fair and adequate compensation. The provision seeks to ensure that expropriated property owners are compensated in line with the legal principle of equivalent reinstatement. Compensation is, therefore, the amount required, so far as money can do so, to put the expropriated owner in the same position as if their property had not been acquired. Literally, it means that affected persons are to be put back in a situation as if nothing had happened to them. Therefore, the payment of a lump sum that is assessed in monetary terms and on a market basis to an expropriated owner to acquire a similar property constitutes fair and adequate compensation.

The Constitution further provides under Article 20 (2) (b) that an aggrieved person shall have access to the high court for redress on matters of ownership rights and quantum of compensation. Section 4 of Act 125 as amended under Act 586 provides the following four explicit legal requirements for a valid claim:

1 Particulars of claim or interest in land.
2 The manner in which his claim or interest has been affected by the instrument.

3 The extent of any damage done.
4 The amount of compensation claimed and the basis for the calculation of the compensation.

However, an unexplored area of specific interest to Valuers or Appraisers is the claimants' noncompliance with the basic requirements of a valid claim. Non-compliance with one or more of these requirements is common. However, when valuation reports are submitted in support of claims, they tend to satisfy the requirements.

The time limit for the service of claim has always remained definite. Valid claims are to be served within six months from the date of publication of the instrument. The Lands Commission, upon receipt of the compensation claim, assesses the quantum of fair and adequate compensation to be paid to the owner of the land acquired.

In assessing the compensation payable, the amendment of Section 4 of Act 125 in Act 586 provides under section 2 (3) that regard shall be had to:

1 The market or replacement value of the land.
2 The cost of disturbance or any other damage suffered thereby.
3 The benefits to be derived by the people of the area in which the land is situated from the use for which the land is acquired.

The market value, the basis of the assessment of compensation, is the value of the acquired land to the owner. The owners' loss shall therefore be tested by the exact value to them and not by what its value will be to the acquiring body. Disturbance is payable as an element of the market value of the land acquired and it has no finite list. It is the balancing factor covering all losses and expenses incurred by a dispossessed owner, provided its claim is incidental and not too remote. Its quantum is directly related to the use, type and location of the acquired property. For commercial properties such as shops and fuel stations, compensation assessment requires additional provision for a specific element of disturbance in the form of goodwill. In some cases, there is compensation for depreciation of land retained and it is usually termed severance. If the depreciation of land refers to that which is caused by what is done on the land taken, it is referred to as injurious affection.

The Valuation Technical Committee of the Lands Commission considers and approves compensation payable. This is followed by two contractual requirements – offer and acceptance – prior to payment. The approved compensation is communicated to the property owner, who is expected to accept or reject it. An accepted offer will be processed for payment. A property owner who declines an offer has to justify and submit a counter claim for negotiation. An agreed upon compensation between the parties is paid but in the event of disagreement, the claimant resorts to the courts for a final determination on the quantum of compensation to be paid.

The date of valuation in determining the quantum of compensation has been contentious because the statutory date is usually the date of the Executive

Instrument whilst in most cases it differs from the date of publication, which in practice could be weeks or months later. Consider the effect on value for money, particularly in an inflationary era. Given these parameters, as it were, and bearing in mind that compensation is not confined merely to what has already happened but extends also to what is expected to happen, the defects may be cured as follows:

1 *Cost of disturbance*: to be based on the date on which the expenses of the change of residence or place of business were actually incurred or would be anticipated.
2 *Other damages*: as this head covers all anticipated injuries likely to result from the execution and use of the works on the land taken, such costs must be genuinely anticipated.
3 *Market value*: the material date of the market value ought to be, first, when the instrument is published. But the value thus ascertained must take into account any benefits enjoyed by the claimant where they remained in possession and in full control of the land after the publication, insofar as it would not be fair or just to require them to do so; or second, where a specific date is stipulated in the Executive Instrument on which the land is to be surrendered to the acquiring body, then the assessment shall be made by reference to that date but where none of the preceding dates apply then; third, the date when possession is taken, which could be after the date of the Executive Instrument but before the date of publication; or fourth, when compensation is assessed and agreed or paid subject to the publication of the Executive Instrument.
4 *Replacement value*: the date when the reinstatement becomes reasonably practicable, but the claim must be submitted within six months following the date of publication of the Executive Instrument.

Underlying these dates is the opinion, logically held, that the land only becomes vested in the president both at law and in equity on the date when notice of publication of the Executive Instrument is made in the Gazette.

A claim served on a government or acquiring body outside the statutory six-month period could be considered out-of-time. Such claims should be processed as compensation to be paid 'ex-gratia,' whether it is grossly out-of-time or not. The 'ex-gratia' could be in quantum the same amount as the compensation would have been and determined by the Land Valuation Division. Claimants under out-of-time cases should forfeit the opportunity to submit a valuation by a private sector Valuer or negotiate a compensation amount.

Involuntary resettlement

The World Bank has developed and implemented policies to regulate payment of compensation for its sponsored projects, particularly in emerging economies. Its operational policies on involuntary resettlement are of specific mention. The World Bank (2007) argues that involuntary resettlement causes severe long-term hardship, impoverishment and environmental damage unless appropriate measures are carefully planned and carried out. For this reason, it permits payment of compensation in the form of loss of business income to Project Affected Persons (PAPs) who may not necessarily have legal or customary interest in affected properties.

Such payments are made to a category of persons where the involuntary taking of landed or other assets results in relocation or loss of shelter; loss of any kind of asset or access to it; and loss of income sources or means of livelihood. Displaced persons are assisted in their efforts to improve their livelihoods and standards of living, and at least to restore them, in real terms, to pre-displacement levels or to levels prevailing prior to the beginning of project implementation, whichever is higher. The closest provisions in the statutes on these reliefs can be found in the Minerals and Mining Act, 2006 (Act 703).

However, a review of Act 703 provides a divergent view that compensation includes an amount for deprivation of the use or a particular use of the natural surface of the land or part of it – loss of or damage to immovable properties. In the case of land under cultivation, it may include loss of earnings or sustenance suffered by the owner or lawful occupier, having due regard to the nature of their interest in the land, and loss of expected income, depending on the nature of crops on the land and their life expectancy. Certainly, the recipient of the compensation may have been deprived of an interest in a landed property.

Rural and urban case studies

Compulsory acquisition and compensation payment for two major national development projects are discussed herein to provide further insight. The Atuabo Gas project in the Western Region is the rural case study. Following the oil and gas discovery in commercial quantities, the Ghana National Gas Company (GNGC) was formed in July 2011 to give a true meaning to government's emphasis on 'local content' in the oil and gas industry. Its primary objective was to build, own and operate the infrastructure required for the gathering, processing, transporting and marketing of natural gas resources. The offshore pipeline, onshore pipeline, gas processing plant, natural gas liquids (NGLs) export system and the office complex were to be established.

The site for the plants and pipeline corridor was acquired following the publication of seven Executive Instruments (E. Is.) – 47, 48, 49, 50, 51, 52 and 53, all in 2014. Acquired sites spanned across seven districts in the region, from Atuabo to Aboadze, covering 111 kilometres and a width of 35 metres. Construction of the gas processing plant at Atuabo and the pipeline also affected seven districts and covered a land size of 910.03 acres. Plant sites were however, spread across five communities covering 1,080.157 acres. Compensation assessment by the Land Valuation Division in respect of 3,683 claimants was deemed fair and reasonable. An equivalent of US$ 5,171,917 as of December 2016 was paid as compensation for crops with no objections. For buildings and structures, only two out of 155 claimants rejected their compensation offers, representing

1.3 percent. Following reviews and negotiation of the rejected offers, the final compensation paid increased from US$ 473,248 to US$ 480,425 (in local currency), representing a 1.5 percent increase in compensation.

Within an urban context, analysis was made in respect of the Millennium Development Authority (MiDA) funded project in Accra, the national capital. The project involved the acquisition of a 14.2 - kilometre stretch of land under Executive Instrument 93 of 2007 for the construction of a three-lane dual carriage between Tetteh Quarshie Interchange and Mallam Junction. This highway is popularly called the George W. Bush Highway or N1 Road. The project, which was completed in December 2011, displaced 11,000 people, affected over 2,632 permanent and temporary buildings and structures, realigned 14.2 kilometres of pipelines and electric cables and relocated 11 fuel filling stations. The entire project was funded from a US$ 557 million compact between the governments of US and Ghana through the Millennium Development Authority.

Only 33 PAPs rejected their compensation offers and submitted counterclaims through their Valuers. Figure 7.1 plots the quantum of compensation recommended by the Land Valuation Division (on behalf of government), private sector Valuers for expropriated property owners and the agreed compensation for payment. For most of the assets valued, compensation values offered by the Land Valuation Division fell below those determined by the private Valuers, whilst agreed figures 'sat' between the two values as clearly shown in Figure 7.1. Six of such compensation values were almost equal in quantum for assessments by both government and private sector Valuers. Agreed compensations paid were therefore significantly not different from the initial offers.

In most cases, valuations confirm the quantum of compensation assessed and offered by the government were fair and reasonable. The findings suggest that as government Valuers, the division is most likely to offer 'floor' values

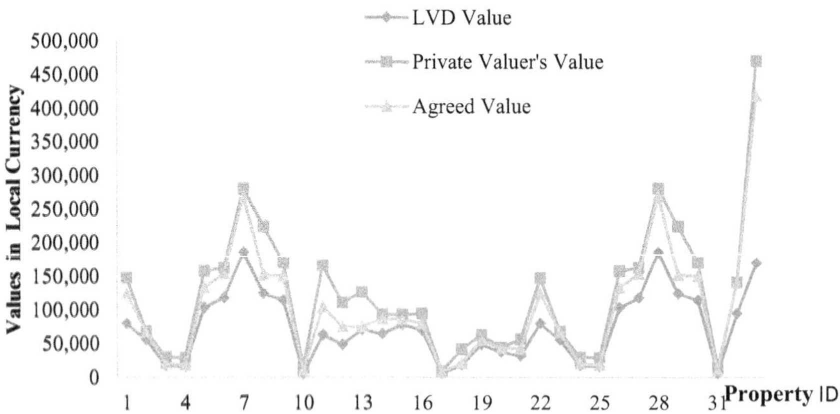

Figure 7.1 Quantum of compensation – by LVD, private Valuers and agreed values

to allow for further negotiations and make savings for the state. The MiDA project produced compensation figures that strongly suggest values obtained by government Valuers and private sector Valuers for the same properties were highly correlated.

The Atuabo Gas and MiDA projects have therefore yielded significant indicators to guide valuation and compensation policy formulation in the country. Valuation skills, experience, and the law and use of appropriate techniques should form the bedrock of compulsory acquisition and compensation with the view to achieving fair and adequate compensation. Prompt payment of compensation nonetheless depends on the availability of funds. This has adequately been provided for in the new Land Act, 2020, but enforcement of the law, at all times, remains indispensable.

References

Adair, A. S., Allen, S., Berry, J. and McGreal, S. (2004). *The development of land and property markets in Central and Eastern Europe: Issues of data*. London: RICS Foundation.

Administration of Lands Act, 1962 (Act 123), Ghana.

Anim-Odame, W. (2009). *Residential real estate investment in emerging economies: The case of Ghana*. Unpublished PhD Thesis, Cass Business School, Faculty of Finance, City University, London.

Anim-Odame, W. (2016). Compulsory acquisition and compensation in Ghana: Principles and practices. *Journal of Business and Estate Management Research*, 1 (1), pp. 11–24. 27th Annual Conference of the American Real Estate Society, Seattle, California, USA, April 13–16, 2011.

Denyer-Green, B. (1998). *Compulsory purchase and compensation*. 5th ed. London: Estates Gazette.

Epstein, R. (1985). *Takings: Private property and the power of eminent domain*. Cambridge, MA: Harvard University Press.

Erasmus, G. (1990). *Compensation for expropriation: A comparative study*. Oxford: The United Kingdom National Committee of Comparative Law.

Johnson, T., Davies, K. and Shapiro, E. (2000). *Modern methods of valuation*. 9th ed. London: Estates Gazette.

Knetsch, J. (1983). *Property rights and compensation: Compulsory acquisition and other losses*. London: Butterworth.

Kotey, N. (2002). Compulsory acquisition of land in Ghana: Does the 1992 constitution open new vistas? In: C. Toulmin, P. Delville and S. Traore ed. *The dynamics of resource tenure in West Africa*. Oxford: James Currey.

Land Act (Act), 2020. Ghana.

Land Valuation Division. (2012). *Valuation standards and guidelines*. Accra: Land Valuation Division.

Mackmin, D. and Emary, R. (2000). The assessment of worth: The need for standards. *Journal of Property Valuation and Investment*, 18 (1).

Minerals and Mining Act, 2006 (Act 703), Ghana.

Republic of Ghana. (1992). *Constitution of the Republic of Ghana*. Accra: Assembly Press, Ghana Publishing Company Limited.

Royal Institution of Chartered Surveyors. (2018). *Valuation standards*. Coventry: Royal Institution of Chartered Surveyors.

Scarrett, D. (1991). *Property valuation: The 5 methods*. London: E & FN Spon.

Scarrett, D. and Osborn, S. (2014). *Property valuation: The five methods*. 3rd ed. London: Routledge.

Stamp Duty (Amendment) Act, 2008 (Act 764), Ghana.

State Lands Act, 1962 (Act 125), Ghana.

State Lands Act, 2000 (Act 586), Ghana.

Whitehead, C. (1983). The rationale for government intervention. In: H. Dunkerly ed., *Urban land policy: Issues and opportunities*. Oxford: Oxford University Press.

World Bank. (2007). *Operational policies on involuntary resettlement*. Washington, DC: The World Bank.

Appendix

Lands Commission checklist for title and deeds registration

A. List of key services

1. Application for regional number/examination data
2. Application for plan approval
3. Application for reprint of already approved plan
4. Application for stamping (financial instrument)
5. Application for stamping (land cases)
6. Application for stamping (other documents)
7. Application for regularisation of state land
8. Application for consent to assign or sublet state land
9. Application for consent to assign (judicial sale)
10. Application for registration (title)
11. Application for assessment and payment of ground rent
12. Application for objection
13. Application for lease (state land)
14. Application for caveat or restriction
15. Application for deeds registration
16. Application for official/administration search
17. Application for certificate search
18. Application for permit search
19. Application for certified true copy
20. Application for substituted certificate
21. Collection of completed application

B. Checklist

1. APPLICATION FOR REGIONAL NUMBER/EXAMINATION DATA

    a. Application on letterhead of licensed surveyor addressed to director, survey and mapping division or their representative
    b. Full name of licensed surveyor's client
    c. Region, district and locality of parcel
    d. Three (3) control points to be used as points of departure and closure
    e. Licensed surveyor's signature

f. Licensed surveyor's number
g. Contacts/telephone number of licensed surveyor
h. Date of letter

2. APPLICATION FOR PLAN APPROVAL

The computation file must contain the following:

a. Application on letterhead of licensed surveyor addressed to Director, Survey and Mapping Division or their representative
b. Examination section data (Ex data)
c. Raw data/field data (Rinex Format)
d. GPS processed data and summary (Point List)
e. Beacon Index
f. Bearing and distances computation from computed coordinates
g. Plan data
h. Area computation
i. Diagram of survey
j. History of survey
k. Eight (8) copies of certified site plan
l. All survey records above on CD (Plot file: AutoCAD DXF or shape file)
m. Completed field inspection form
n. File index
o. Regional number for the survey
p. Signature of licensed surveyor
q. Licensed surveyor's number
r. Date of letter
s. Regional number on top right corner of back of file

ADDITIONALLY, LICENSED SURVEYOR MUST SUBMIT BIOGRAPHIC DATA OF LICENSED SURVEYOR'S CLIENT AS FOLLOWS (bio-data form to be obtained at Front Desk of CSAU during application for regional number):

a. Name of licensed surveyor's client
b. Gender of client
c. Nationality of licensed surveyor's client
d. Address/house number of licensed surveyor's client
e. Copy of photo ID of client (passport/voter's ID/driver's license/national ID)
f. Mobile telephone number of licensed surveyor's client
g. E-mail address of licensed surveyor's client (if any)

3. APPLICATION FOR REPRINT OF ALREADY APPROVED PLAN

a. Application on licensed surveyor's letterhead
b. Full name of licensed surveyor's client
c. Regional number of survey
d. Locality name of parcel
e. Eight (8) copies of certified plan for approval

f. Photocopy of already approved plan (if available)

4. APPLICATION FOR STAMPING (FINANCIAL INSTRUMENT)
The financial instrument being submitted for stamping must clearly show the following:

a. Date of instrument
b. Signature of party/parties
c. Notary public seal (mandatory only if document is not original)
d. Consideration of facility

5. APPLICATION FOR STAMPING (LAND CASES)
Please ensure that the document has the following:

a. Title of document clearly stated
b. Date of document
c. Names and addresses of parties
d. Consideration, rent, term/commencement date
e. The following information on site plan must be the same in document:

 i. Name of owner
 ii. Land size and location of land

f. Licensed surveyor's and Director, Survey and Mapping Division's signatures and date
g. Document must be original or certified true copy or photocopy with an affidavit
h. Back of the site plan must be signed by the parties
i. Signature of parties
j. Signature of witnesses of parties with address
k. Jurat (if document is thumbprinted, etc.)
l. Solicitor's seal
m. Oath of proof must be executed
n. Deponent must be completed by grantor's witness

6. APPLICATION FOR STAMPING (OTHER DOCUMENTS)
Please ensure that the document has the following:

a. Date of instrument
b. Signature of part/parties

7. APPLICATION FOR REGULARISATION OF STATE LAND

a. Application letter signed by Applicant/Solicitor/Estate surveyor/their authorised representative with a power of attorney
b. An approved site plan
c. A copy of document granted by the preacquisition owner (optional)/ evidence of occupation
d. A copy of applicant's valid photo ID

OR

A copy of evidence of legal existence (certificate to commence business and incorporation) and certificate of annual renewal plus a copy of photo ID of company's representative

8. APPLICATION FOR CONSENT TO ASSIGN OR SUBLET STATE LAND

   a. Application letter signed by the assignor(s)/sublessor(s) or their authorised representative with a power of attorney
   b. A copy of the draft assignment/sublease document
   c. A copy of the applicant's title document (optional)
   d. A copy of the applicant's valid photo ID
   e. A copy of evidence of legal existence (certificate to commence business and incorporation) and certificate of annual renewal (where assignee/sublessee is a company) plus a copy of photo ID of company's representative
   f. A copy of the company's resolution to assign/sublet (where assignor/sublessor(s) is a company)
   g. An approved site plan clearly showing the subdivision (if part transfer) and a copy of old site plan (if applicant has earlier processed a document with an unapproved plan)
   h. A subdivision approval from Land Use and Spatial Planning Authority (formerly Town and Country Planning Department) with an extract from the layout (if part transfer)

9. APLICATION FOR CONSENT TO ASSIGN (JUDICIAL SALE)

   a. An application letter signed by the registrar of the court
   b. An approved site plan
   c. The certificate of purchase
   d. A copy of applicant's valid photo ID
   e. A copy of evidence of legal existence (certificate to commence business and incorporation) and certificate of annual renewal (where assignee/purchase is a company) plus a copy of photo ID of company's representative
   f. A copy of the judgement based on which property is being transferred
   g. A copy of the deed of assignment from the court

10. APPLICATION FOR REGISTRATION (TITLE)
    The document/instrument being submitted for registration must clearly show the following:

    a. Stamped (stamped duty duly paid)
    b. Date of instrument
    c. Nature of instrument (title of document)
    d. Name and address of parties
    e. Signature of parties

f. Name and address of witnesses
g. Signature of witnesses
h. Solicitor's stamp/seal
i. Approved plan (certified judgement plan if nature of instrument is judgement)
j. The following information on site plan must be the same in the document:

    i. Name of owner
    ii. Land size and location of land

k. Licensed surveyor's and Director, Survey and Mapping Division's signatures and date
l. Back of the site plan must be signed by the parties
m. Signature of witnesses of parties with addresses
n. Jurat (if document is thumbprinted, etc.)
o. Oath of proof must be executed
p. Deponent must be completed by grantor's witnesses
q. Planning comments/approval with extracts from layout from the Land Use and Spatial Planning Authority (formerly Town and Country Planning Department) (for stool lands only)
r. All supporting/recited documents must be attached
s. Evidence of concurrence/consent (stool and state lands subsequent transactions)
t. Original land certificate of transferor (for transfer of whole)

11. APPLICATION FOR ASSESSMENT AND PAYMENT OF GROUND RENT

    a. An application indicating where the land is located as well as the plot number
    b. Evidence of last payment

12. APPLICATION OF OBJECTION

    a. Letter with basis for the objection
    b. Attach all documentary evidence supporting the objection

13. APPLICATION FOR LEASE (STATE LAND)

    a. An application letter signed by applicant(s)/representative of company
    b. Passport size photograph of applicant(s) or company representative
    c. Completed application form and questionnaire (obtained from CSAU)
    d. Copy of applicants' valid photo ID or photo ID of company's representative
    e. An approved site plan (optional)
    f. A copy of evidence of legal existence (certificate to commence business and incorporation) and certificate of annual renewal (where applicant is a company)

14. APPLICATION FOR CAVEAT OR RESTRICTION

    a. Fill caveat application form with the following details:

        i. Certificate number
        ii. Volume
        iii. Folio
        iv. Plan and survey reference numbers
        v. Particulars of parties
        vi. Date of application
        vii. Basis of the caveat on form
        viii. Signature of applicant

    b. Attach all documentary evidence

15. APPLICATION FOR DEEDS REGISTRATION

    a. Date of instrument
    b. Nature of instrument (title of document)
    c. Name and address of parties
    d. Signature of parties
    e. Name and address of witnesses
    f. Signature of witnesses
    g. Solicitor's stamp/seal
    h. Approved plan
    i. The following information on site plan must be the same in document:

        i. Name of owner
        ii. Land size and location of land

    j. Licensed surveyor's and Director, Survey and Mapping Division's signatures and date
    k. Back of site plan must be signed by the parties
    l. Signature of witnesses of parties with addresses
    m. Jurat (if document is thumbprinted, etc.)
    n. Oath of proof must be executed
    o. Deponent must be completed by grantor's witness
    p. Planning comments/approval with extracts from layout from the Land Use and Spatial Planning Authority (formerly Town and Country Planning Department) (for stool lands)
    q. Tax clearance certificate from Ghana Revenue Authority
    r. All supporting/recited documents must be attached
    s. Submit evidence of payment of ground rent (if not first registration)

16. APPLICATION FOR OFFICIAL/ADMINISTRATIVE SEARCH

    a. An application letter
    b. Two (2) copies of site plans which must meet the following requirements:

    i. The site must be edged pink
    ii. Site plan must have visible grid values and
    iii. Site plan must be drawn to a scale of 1:2500 or any appropriate standard scale

17. APPLICATION FOR CERTIFICATE SEARCH
    a. Fully completed application/affirmation forms
    b. Valid photo ID of applicant/affirmant

    Application and affirmation forms can be obtained at the CSAU.

18. APPLICATION FOR PERMIT SEARCH
    a. Completed application form from the Metro/Municipal/District assembly
    b. Two (2) site plans edged pink
        i. Site plans must have visible grid values and
        ii. Site plans must be drawn to a scale of 1:2500 or any appropriate standard scale

19. APPLICATION FOR CERTIFIED TRUE COPY
    a. An application letter signed by the property owner or their authorised representative with a power of attorney
    b. A copy of a valid photo ID of applicant
    c. An approved site plan (for applications for certified plotted documents)
    d. A police extract (for applications for certified plotted documents)

20. APPLICATION FOR SUBSTITUTED CERTIFICATE
    a. Application letter
    b. Police extract
    c. Photocopy of the publication in the national dailies

21. COLLECTION OF COMPLETED APPLICATIONS
    You will be required to submit the following to collect a completed application:

    APPLICATION FOR REGISTRATION

        a. Photo ID of grantee
        b. Photo ID of collector
        c. Authority note from grantee
        d. Evidence of payment of concurrence (for stool lands)
        e. Evidence of payment of ground rent (for stool and selected family land)

    APPLICATION FOR PLAN APPROVAL

        a. Authority note from licensed surveyor
        b. Photo ID of licensed surveyor
        c. Photo ID of collector

    APPLICATION FOR STAMPING (FINANCIAL INSTRUMENT)

        a. Photo ID of bank's or company's representative
        b. Authority note from bank or company

APPLICATION FOR STAMPING (all other documents)

a. Photo ID of grantee
b. Authority note from grantee
c. Photo ID of collector

APPLICATION FOR MORTGAGES

a. Photo ID of collector
b. Authority note from the bank

Index

Note: Page numbers in **bold** indicate a table on the corresponding page.

www.ingramcontent.com/pod-product-compliance
Lightning Source LLC
LaVergne TN
LVHW021111300926
849160LV00009B/692
* 9 7 8 0 3 6 7 6 7 2 5 2 2 *